LIGHTHOUSE REVIEW

The Ultimate Math Refresher Workbook

Published by Lighthouse Review, Inc., Austin, Texas 78716

Lighthouse Review, Inc.
The Ultimate Math Refresher Workbook

ISBN: 0-9677594-0-4

CONTENTS

RELATED PUBLICATIONS

Are you taking the LSAT, GRE, GMAT, or SAT? If so, check out the comprehensive review materials published by Lighthouse Review, Inc.

LSAT. The *Lighthouse LSAT Prep Self-Study Course* is a well organized, challenging study program which has been carefully designed to prepare students for the LSAT. The program is organized by question type. Each section contains detailed expository materials, summaries of important concepts and procedures and timed practice exercises. Detailed written explanations follow each exercise. The course includes an up-to-date 350 page textbook, two full, simulated LSATs, a complete study plan and access to our telephone help-line.

GRE. The *Lighthouse GRE Prep Self-Study Course* is a well organized, challenging study program which has been carefully designed to prepare students for the GRE. The program is organized by question type. Each section contains detailed expository materials, summaries of important concepts and procedures and timed practice exercises. Detailed written explanations follow each exercise.The course includes a 500 page textbook, this Math Refresher Workbook, a 175 page Vocabulary Refresher Workbook, a full, simulated GRE, a complete study plan and access to our telephone help-line.

GMAT. The *Lighthouse GMAT Prep Self-Study Course* is a well organized, challenging study program which has been carefully designed to prepare students for the GMAT. The program is organized by question type. Each section contains detailed expository materials, summaries of important concepts and procedures and timed practice exercises. Detailed written explanations follow each exercise. The course includes an up-to-date 500 page textbook, this Math Refresher Workbook, three full, simulated GMATs, a detailed step-by-step study plan and access to our telephone help-line.

SAT. The *Lighthouse SAT Prep Self-Study Course* stresses fundamentals and provides in-depth instruction that you can master at you own pace. Your SAT score is too important for you to walk into the test unprepared. SAT now stands for Scholastic Assessment Test. This change highlights the fact that the SAT is not a test of intelligence, but rather a test of skills. That's why Lighthouse provides techniques and skills exercises in a well organized, challenging study program.

The program is organized by question type. Each section contains detailed expository materials, summaries of important concepts and procedures and timed practice exercises. Detailed written explanations follow each exercise. The course includes a 500 page textbook, this Math Refresher Workbook, a 175 page Vocabulary Refresher Workbook, a full, simulated SAT, a complete study plan and access to our telephone help-line.

To learn more information about our programs, go to our website at www.lighthousereview.com, drop us an e-mail at info@lighthousereview.com, call us at (512) 306-9701, send us a facsimile at (512) 328-4137, or write us at Lighthouse Review, Inc., P.O. Box 160205, Austin, Texas 78716-0205.

MATHEMATICS REVIEW

Introduction

This math refresher workbook is designed to clearly and concisely state the basic math rules and principles which you need to master. The most important feature of this math review is a series of carefully sequenced practice sets designed to build your math skills step-by-step. Because our goal is to help you efficiently acquire the knowledge and skills you need, we have tried to keep the text as spare as possible by focusing on the practice problems and their solutions.

Format. It is important to note that the problems included in this book are *not* in test format. The major difference is that it is up to you to work out the solution to each question because the questions do not have answer choices. Later, you will find that the answer choices are the key to solving many problems in test format because you can often use the answer choices to reach a solution indirectly. This math refresher course emphasizes basic concepts and problem solving skills. Strategies for specific question types in test format are the focus of the *Lighthouse Review* Self Study programs.

Important procedures. The following procedures are suggested in order to help you obtain maximum benefit from this math review:

1. Focus on the practice sets first and foremost. Acquiring new skills will require hard work. Having a "general understanding" of a topic is a poor substitute for actually working the problems. You owe it to yourself to prove your knowledge by *working the problems*. If you carefully complete each practice set (there are a total of 34 practice sets) you will be ready to master the strategies for specific question types in test format.

2. Avoid use of a calculator even for simple calculations. By working each step manually you will build your skills and will learn to avoid careless mistakes.

PART 1: ARITHMETIC

Numbers

Symbols Chart

It is important that you recognize the following mathematical symbols:

$=$	equals
$\neq$	does not equal
$\approx$	approximately equals
$>$	is greater than
$<$	is less than
$\geq$	is greater than or equal to
$\leq$	is less than or equal to
x^2	x squared
$\sqrt{x}$	square root of x
$\parallel$	is parallel to
$\perp$	is perpendicular to
π	pi (≈ 3.14)
$\triangle$	triangle
$\angle$	angle
$|x|$	the absolute value of x

Number Line

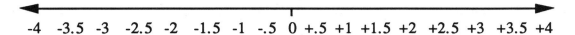

-4   -3.5   -3   -2.5   -2   -1.5   -1   -.5   0   +.5   +1   +1.5   +2   +2.5   +3   +3.5   +4

All *real* numbers can be expressed as points on a number line. On the number line above, the point furthest left represents -4, while the point furthest right represents +4. Number lines are useful in the determination of relative values. Each point to the left of 0 is negative (such points are *negative* signed numbers). Each point to the right of 0 is positive (such points are *positive* signed numbers).

If we wanted to take the *absolute value* of the numbers represented on the number line discussed above, we would simply extract each number from its sign. The absolute value of the point furthest left would therefore be the same as the absolute value of the point furthest right. This reflects the fact that -4 and +4 are equidistant from 0, the *origin*. Absolute value is denoted via the placement of a vertical line on either side of a number: $|-4| = 4$ and $|4| = 4$.

Numbers on the line get progressively greater with movement to the right, and progressively smaller with movement to the left. The *integers* or *whole* numbers on the line above are: -4, -3, -2, -1, 0, 1, 2, 3 and 4. Integers are evenly divisible by 1. *Consecutive* integers are just that, integers that follow consecutively—in regular increasing order. Thus -2, -1, 0, 1 and 2 are consecutive integers. On the other hand, 1 and 3 are not consecutive integers. Real numbers can be *rational* (numbers that can be expressed as the quotient of two integers such as whole numbers or fractions) or *irrational* (numbers that cannot be expressed as the quotient of integers or functions such as π and $\sqrt{2}$). Recall that all real numbers can be expressed as points on a number line. For instance, π, which is approximately 3.14, would fit between 3 and 3.5 on the number line above. Similarly, $\sqrt{2}$, which is approximately 1.4, would fit between 1 and 1.5.

Zero

Four things to remember about zero:

1. Adding zero to any number results in that number:

    $3 + 0 = 3$

2. Subtracting zero from any number results in that number:

    $3 - 0 = 3$

3. Multiplying any number by zero results in zero:

    $3 \times 0 = 0$

4. Dividing any number by zero is not possible:

    $3 \div 0 =$ undefined

Signed Numbers

Six things to remember about operations with signed numbers:

1. To add two like signed numbers, add the absolute value of the numbers and keep the sign:

    $3 + 2 = 5$

    and

    $-3 + -2 = -5$

2. To add two unlike signed numbers, subtract the absolute value of the smaller number from the absolute value of the larger number and keep the sign of the number with the larger absolute value:

    $4 + -2 = 2$

    but

    $-4 + 2 = -2$

3. To multiply two like signed numbers, multiply the absolute values. The sign will always be positive:

    $3 \times 2 = 6$

    and

    $-3 \times -2 = 6$

4. To multiply two unlike signed numbers, multiply the absolute values and add a negative sign:

    $8 \times -4 = -32$

5. To divide two like signed numbers, divide the absolute values. The sign will always be positive:

    $6 \div 3 = 2$

    and

    $-6 \div -3 = 2$

6. To divide two unlike signed numbers, divide the absolute values and add a negative sign:

    $-8 \div 4 = -2$

Odds and Ends

If you are *adding* more than two signed numbers, do so by adding any two of the numbers and then adding the result to another of the numbers and so on until the final result is reached *or* add all the positive numbers together and all the negative numbers together and proceed as in 2 above.

If you are *multiplying* more than two signed numbers at a time, simply multiply the absolute values of two of the numbers and then multiply the result by the absolute value of another of the numbers and so on until the final result is reached. Then count the number of negative terms. If the resulting number is *odd* (that is; not divisible by 2), then the sign of the product is *negative*. Conversely, if the resulting number of negative terms is *even* (that is; divisible by 2), then the sign of the product is *positive*. These methods are derived from some basic principles of even and odd integers (principles which *can* save you time):

an even plus an even equals an even	$2 + 6 = 8$	and	$-2 + 6 = 4$
an odd plus an odd equals an even	$5 + 7 = 12$	and	$-5 + -7 = -12$
an odd plus an even equals an odd	$5 + 4 = 9$	and	$-5 + 4 = -1$
an even minus an even equals an even	$6 - 4 = 2$	and	$-6 - 4 = -10$
an odd minus an odd equals an even	$7 - 3 = 4$	and	$-7 + 3 = -4$
an odd minus an even equals an odd	$9 - 6 = 3$	and	$-9 - 6 = -15$
an even minus an odd equals an odd	$8 - 3 = 5$	and	$-8 - 3 = -11$
an even times an even equals an even	$2 \times 4 = 8$	and	$-2 \times -4 = 8$
an odd times an odd equals an odd	$3 \times 7 = 21$	and	$-3 \times 7 = -21$
an odd times an even equals an even	$4 \times 7 = 28$	and	$4 \times -7 = -28$

PRACTICE SET 1

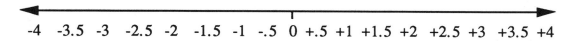

-4   -3.5 -3   -2.5 -2   -1.5 -1 -.5 0 +.5 +1 +1.5 +2 +2.5 +3 +3.5 +4

1.   Determine if the following relations are true or false:

   a. $3 > 2$

   b. $1 > 2$

   c. $-3 > -2$

   d. $-1 > 2$

2. What is the next consecutive integer after 2?

3. What is the next consecutive integer after -2?

4. Solve the following:

    a. $7 + 5 =$

    b. $7 - 5 =$

    c. $-7 + 5 =$

    d. $-7 - 5 =$

    e. $0 - 4 =$

    f. $0 \times -4 =$

    g. $6 \times 9 =$

    h. $6 \times -9 =$

    i. $-6 \times 9 =$

    j. $-6 \times -9 =$

    k. $-2 \times 3 \times -4 =$

5. If two negative numbers are multiplied, what is the sign of the product?

6. If an odd number is added to an even number, what can be said with certainty about their sum?

7. If an odd, positive number and an even, negative number are multiplied, what can be said with certainty about their product?

ANSWERS—PRACTICE SET 1

1. a. T
   b. F
   c. F
   d. F

2. 3

3. -1

4. a. 12
   b. 2
   c. -2
   d. -12
   e. -4
   f. 0
   g. 54
   h -54
   i. -54
   j. 54
   k. 24

5. positive

6. odd

7. The product will be even and negative.

Order of Operations

Suppose you are asked to find the value of $3 + 82 \times 9 - (16 + 4 - 3 \times 6) \div 2$. Where would you start? Don't fret, just remember the following mnemonic:

PEMDAS = Please Excuse My Dear Aunt Sally (a grade school stand-by)

P   stands for   parentheses   (parentheses within parentheses take priority)

E   stands for   exponents

M   stands for   multiplication (multiply and divide in order from left to right)

D   stands for   division

A   stands for   addition   (add and subtract in order from left to right)

S   stands for   subtraction

To solve problems which require you to perform more than one operation at a time:

(1) get rid of parentheses (attend to parentheses within parentheses first)
(2) get rid of exponents
(3) perform multiplications and divisions in order from left to right
(4) perform additions and subtractions in order from left to right

(Please note that operations with exponents are dealt with in a subsequent section and thus will not appear in the sample questions and practice set that immediately follow.)

Sample Question 1: $3 + 82 \times 9 - (16 + 4 - 3 \times 6) \div 2 = ?$

Process (words)	Process (numbers)
(1) eliminate the parentheses	(1) $3 + 82 \times 9 - (16 + 4 - 18) \div 2$
	$3 + 82 \times 9 - (20 - 18) \div 2$
	$3 + 82 \times 9 - 2 \div 2$
(2) eliminate exponents	(2) not applicable
(3) multiply and divide	(3) $3 + 738 - 1$
(4) add and subtract	(4) $741 - 1$
	740

Sample Question 2: $59 \times 32 + (45 + (6 \div 3 \times 4) - 8) \div 5 = ?$

Process (words)	Process (numbers)
(1) eliminate the parentheses	(1) $59 \times 32 + (45 + 8 - 8) \div 5$
	$59 \times 32 + 45 \div 5$
(2) eliminate exponents	(2) not applicable
(3) multiply and divide	(3) $1888 + 9$
(4) add and subtract	(4) 1897

Three Laws of Operations

Here are three laws which can be used to simplify operations:

1. Commutative: This law says that like operations (additions or multiplications only) can be performed in any order. For instance $6 + 12$ is the same thing as $12 + 6$ and 8×2 is the same thing as 2×8.

2. Associative: This law says that like operations (additions or multiplications only) can be regrouped in any order. For instance $25 + 30 + 75 + 70$ is easier dealt with as $(25 + 75) + (30 + 70)$ and $10 \times 12 \times 15 \times 12$ is easier dealt with as $(10 \times 15) \times (12 \times 12)$.

3. Distributive: This law says that it's okay to distribute a factor across terms being added or subtracted. For instance $3(2 + 22)$ is $(3 \times 2) + (3 \times 22)$ is $(6 + 66)$ or 72, and $4(8 - 3)$ is $(4 \times 8) - (4 \times 3)$ is $(32 - 12)$ or 20.

These laws are to be used in conjunction with PEMDAS. At times, you can get rid of the parentheses indirectly, by using the distributive law first. You might also perform a series of additions or multiplications within a set of parentheses in backwards order (from right to left).

Sample Question 3: $6(10 + 6) \times 8 + 3(16 + 18) = ?$

<u>Process (words)</u>	<u>Process (numbers)</u>
(1) use the distributive law	(1) $(60 + 36) \times 8 + (48 + 54)$
(2) eliminate parentheses	$96 \times 8 + 102$
(3) eliminate exponents	(2) not applicable
(4) multiply and divide	(3) $768 + 102$
(5) add and subtract	(4) 870

On occasion ETS uses another method of grouping besides parenthesis. The "absolute" value of an expression is simply the positive value of the expression. For instance, $|2| = 2$ and $|-2| = 2$. To eliminate the absolute value signs, simply solve the inside expression and take the positive value:

$$3|3 - 7| = 3|-4|$$
$$= 3 \times 4$$
$$= 12$$

PRACTICE SET 2

1. $-(3-5) =$

2. $2 + 8 \times 4 =$

3. $(2 + 8) \times 4 =$

4. $5 + 2(8 - 3) =$

5. $-(5 + 2)(8 - 3) =$

6. $(5 + (2)(8)) - 3 =$

7. $17 + 3(7 - (4 + 2)) =$

8. $24 \div (2 + (-12 \div 3)) =$

9. $500 - (7 + (-2 - (11 - 2 \times 3))) =$

10. $(7 \times 3 - 21)(7 \times 3 + 21) =$

11. $|20 - 14| - |14 - 20| =$

12. $4|-3(7 - 2)| =$

16

ANSWERS AND EXPLANATIONS—PRACTICE SET 2

1. 2 $\quad -(3-5) = -3+5$
$$= 2$$

2. 34 $\quad 2+8\times 4 = 2+32$
$$= 34$$

3. 40 $\quad (2+8)\times 4 = 10\times 4$
$$= 40$$

4. 15 $\quad 5+2(8-3) = 5+2(5)$
$$= 5+10$$
$$= 15$$

5. −35 $\quad -(5+2)(8-3) = (-5-2)(5)$
$$= (-7)(5)$$
$$= -35$$

6. 18 $\quad (5+(2)(8))-3 = (5+16)-3$
$$= 21-3$$
$$= 18$$

7. 20 $\quad 17+3(7-(4+2)) = 17+3(7-6)$
$$= 17+3(1)$$
$$= 17+3$$
$$= 20$$

8. −12 $\quad 24\div(2+(-12\div 3)) = 24\div(2+(-4))$
$$= 24\div(2-4)$$
$$= 24\div -2$$
$$= -12$$

9. 500 $\quad 500-(7+(-2-(11-2\times 3))) = 500-(7+(-2-(11-6)))$
$$= 500-(7+(-2-5))$$
$$= 500-(7+(-7))$$
$$= 500-0$$
$$= 500$$

10. 0 $(7 \times 3 - 21)(7 \times 3 + 21) = (21 - 21)(21 + 21)$
$$= (0)(42)$$
$$= 0$$

11. 0 $|20 - 14| - |14 - 20| = |6| - |-6|$
$$= 6 - 6$$
$$= 0$$

12. 60 $4|-3(7 - 2)| = 4|-3(5)|$
$$= 4|-15|$$
$$= 4(15)$$
$$= 60$$

Prime and Composite Numbers

Prime numbers, like 2, 3 and 11, have only two divisors, themselves and one. Most numbers, however, have more than two divisors, and are called *composite* numbers. 6, 24 and 45 are composite numbers. All composite numbers can be written as a product of their *prime factors*. Prime factors of composite numbers are easily determined with factor trees. Here are factor trees for 6, 8 and 15 (although other trees are possible):

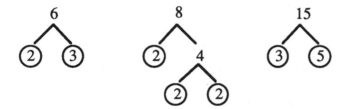

As you can see, the first branch consists of two numbers whose product is the given number. The branching process goes on until the number at the end of each branch is prime. The collection of circled numbers under any one of the above numbers represents the *prime factorization* of that number. You may be asked to find "the number of *distinct* prime factors" of a given number, say 325. Since distinct prime factors means different prime factors, you would simply count each different prime number at the end of the factor tree for that given number. Since 325 = 5 × 5 × 13, 325 has three prime factors, two of which are distinct (5 is not distinct from 5). Neither 0 nor 1 is considered prime. Here are all of the prime numbers under 50:

2, 3, 5, 7, 11, 13, 17, 19, 23, 29, 31, 37, 41, 43, 47

Note that 2 is the only even prime number listed above. It is in fact the *only* even prime number.

Numbers, both prime and composite, have a limitless number of *multiples*; that is, integers that are divisible by them. 8 and 12 are multiples of the composite number 4. 25, 60 and 100 are multiples of the prime number 5. In fact, the product of any integer multiplied by 4 is a

18

multiple of 4 and the product of any integer multiplied by 5 is a multiple of 5. What, though, would be the *least common multiple* of 4 and 5?

To find the least common multiple between two numbers:

(1) factor both numbers using a prime factoring tree
(2) circle all the factors of the first number
(3) eliminate any factors in the second number which repeat factors in the first number, and circle those that remain
(4) multiply the circled factors

Sample Question 4: The least common multiple of 4 and 5 = ?

Process (words)	Process (numbers)
(1) prime factor both numbers	(1) $4 = 2 \times 2$
	$5 = 5$
(2) circle (brackets) factors of first number	(2) $4 = [2] \times [2]$
(3) eliminate repeating factors in second number and circle (brackets) those that remain	(3) $5 = [5]$ (none repeat)
(4) multiply circled factors	(4) $2 \times 2 \times 5 = 20$

Sample Question 5: The least common multiple of 20 and 45 = ?

Process (words)	Process (numbers)
(1) prime factor both numbers	(1) $20 = 5 \times 2 \times 2$
	$45 = 5 \times 3 \times 3$
(2) circle (brackets) factors of first number	(2) $20 = [5] \times [2] \times [2]$
(3) eliminate repeating factors in second number and circle (brackets) those that remain	(3) $45 = 5 \times [3] \times [3]$ (5 repeats)
(4) multiply circled factors	(4) $5 \times 2 \times 2 \times 3 \times 3 = 180$

Composite numbers can have factors other than their prime factors, as is evidenced by the middle branches of the factor trees. Each positive integer that evenly divides into a number is a *factor* of that number. The factors of 6 are 1, 2, 3 and 6. The factors of 8 are 1, 2, 4, and 8. The factors of 15 are 1, 3, 5, and 15. The factors of 325 are 1, 5, 13, 25, 65 and 325.

PRACTICE SET 3

1. Determine the prime factors of the following numbers:

    a. 12

    b. 60

    c. 78

    d. 125

    e. 140

    f. 69

    g. 138

    h. 31

2. What is the number of distinct prime factors of the following numbers?

    a. 78

    b. 125

    c. 60

3. Is 138 a multiple of 23? of 69?

4. Is 78 a multiple of 12?

5. What is the LCM of 15 and 90?

6. What is the LCM of 28 and 80?

7. Is the LCM of 33 and 110 even or odd?

8. What is the LCM of 198 and 495?

20

ANSWERS—PRACTICE SET 3

1. a. $2 \times 2 \times 3$
    b. $2 \times 2 \times 3 \times 5$
    c. $2 \times 3 \times 13$
    d. $5 \times 5 \times 5$
    e. $2 \times 2 \times 5 \times 7$
    f. 3×23
    g. $2 \times 3 \times 23$
    h. 31 is a prime number, it cannot be factored.

2. a. 3 Refer to (c) in question 1. 78 has 3 distinct prime factors.
    b. 1 Refer to (d) in question 1. 125 has 1 distinct prime factor.
    c. 3 Refer to (b) in question 1. 60 has 3 distinct prime factors.

3. yes, yes 138 is a multiple of 23 if 23 divides evenly into 138. $138 \div 23 = 6$, so 138 is a multiple of 23. $138 \div 69 = 2$, so 138 is also a multiple of 12.

4. no $78 \div 12 = 6.5$, so 78 is not a multiple of 12.

5. 90

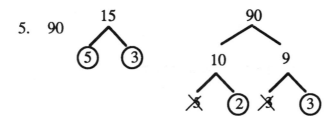

$$5 \times 3 \times 2 \times 3 = 90$$

Note that we can only eliminate one of the 3's in the second tree, because we've circled only one 3 in the first tree. Always use this one-for-one method when figuring lowest common multiple.

6. 560

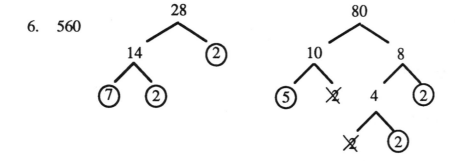

$$7 \times 2 \times 2 \times 5 \times 2 \times 2 = 560$$

There are two 2's in the first tree, so we eliminate only two 2's in the second tree.

7. even (330)

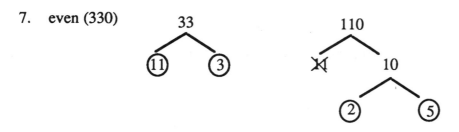

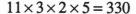

$$11 \times 3 \times 2 \times 5 = 330$$

8. 990

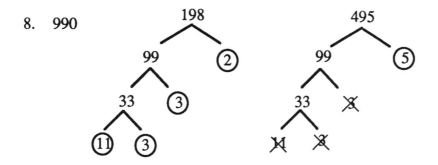

$$11 \times 3 \times 3 \times 2 \times 5 = 990$$

Tests of Divisibility

Here are seven useful tests of divisibility:

1. A number is evenly divisible by <u>2</u> if its unit's digit (its last digit) is divisible by 2. 4 is divisible by 2, and so is 3,000,258.

2. A number is evenly divisible by <u>3</u> if the sum of its digits is divisible by 3. 36 is divisible by 3 and so is 87,798.

3. A number is evenly divisible by <u>4</u> if the number made by the ten's and the unit's digits (the last two digits) is divisible by 4. 116 is divisible by 4 and so is 548,988.

4. A number is evenly divisible by <u>5</u> if its unit's digit (its last digit) is a 0 or a 5. 65 is divisible by 5 and so is 324,560.

5. A number is evenly divisible by <u>6</u> if it is divisible by both 2 and 3 (its unit's digit is divisible by 2 and if the sum of its digits is divisible by 3). 510 is divisible by 6 and so is 6,534.

6. A number is evenly divisible by <u>9</u> if the sum of its digits is divisible by 9. 135 is divisible by 9 and so is 410,985.

7. A number is evenly divisible by <u>10</u> if its unit's digit is a zero. 20 is divisible by 10 and so is 112,990.

PRACTICE SET 4

Test the following numbers for even divisibility by 2, 3, 4, 5, 6, 9 and 10.

1. 2,000

2. 1,372

3. 22,542

4. 415,701

5. 121,945

6. 243,890

7. 7,442

8. 19,683

9. 1,048,576

10. 1,555,200

ANSWERS AND EXPLANATIONS—PRACTICE SET 4

1. [2, 4, 5, 10] 2,000 is evenly divisible by 2 because its unit's digit (0) is evenly divisible by 2. 2,000 is not evenly divisible by 3 because the sum of its digits (2) is not evenly divisible by 3. 2,000 is evenly divisible by 4 because the number made by its last two digits (0) is evenly divisible by 4. 2,000 is evenly divisible by 5 because its unit's digits (0) is a 0 or a 5. 2,000 is not evenly divisible by 6 because it is not evenly divisible by both 2 and 3. 2,000 is not evenly divisible by 9 because the sum of its digits (2) is not evenly divisible by 9. 2,000 is evenly divisible by 10 because its unit's digit is a 0.

2. [2, 4] 1,372 is evenly divisible by 2 because its unit's digit (2) is evenly divisible by 2. 1,372 is not evenly divisible by 3 because the sum of its digits (13) is not evenly divisible by 3. 1,372 is evenly divisible by 4 because the number made by its last two digits (72) is evenly divisible by 4. 1,372 is not evenly divisible by 5 because its unit's digits (2) is not a 0 or a 5. 1,372 is not evenly divisible by 6 because it is not evenly divisible by both 2 and 3. 1,372 is not evenly divisible by 9 because the sum of its digits (13) is not evenly divisible by 9. 1,372 is not evenly divisible by 10 because its unit's digits is not a 0.

3. [2, 3, 6] 22,542 is evenly divisible by 2 because its unit's digit (2) is evenly divisible by 2. 22,542 is evenly divisible by 3 because the sum of its digits (15) is evenly divisible by 3. 22,542 is not evenly divisible by 4 because the number made by its last two digits (42) is not evenly divisible by 4. 22,542 is not evenly divisible by 5 because its unit's digits (2) is not a 0 or a 5. 22,542 is evenly divisible by 6 because it is evenly divisible by both 2 and 3. 22,542 is not evenly divisible by 9 because the sum of its digits (15) is not evenly divisible by 9. 22,542 is not evenly divisible by 10 because its unit's digit (2) is not a 0.

4. [3, 9] 415,701 is not evenly divisible by 2 because its unit's digit (1) is not evenly divisible by 2. 415,701 is evenly divisible by 3 because the sum of its digits (18) is evenly divisible by 3. 415,701 is not evenly divisible by 4 because the number made by its last two digits (1) is not evenly divisible by 4. 415,701 is not evenly divisible by 5 because its unit's digits (1) is not a 0 or a 5. 415,701 is not evenly divisible by 6 because it is not evenly divisible by both 2 and 3. 415,701 is evenly divisible by 9 because the sum of its digits (18) is evenly divisible by 9. 415,701 is not evenly divisible by 10 because its unit's digit (1) is not a 0.

5. [5] 121,945 is not evenly divisible by 2 because its unit's digit (5) is not evenly divisible by 2. 121,945 is not evenly divisible by 3 because the sum of its digits (22) is not evenly divisible by 3. 121,945 is not evenly divisible by 4 because the number made by its last two digits (45) is not evenly divisible by 4. 121,945 is evenly divisible by 5 because its unit's digits (5) is a 0 or a 5. 121,945 is not evenly divisible by 6 because it is not evenly divisible by both 2 and 3. 121,945 is not evenly divisible by 9 because the sum of its digits (22) is not evenly divisible by 9. 121,945 is not evenly divisible by 10 because its unit's digit (5) is not a 0.

6. [2, 5, 10] 243,890 is evenly divisible by 2 because its unit's digit (0) is evenly divisible by 2. 243,890 is not evenly divisible by 3 because the sum of its digits (26) is not evenly divisible by 3. 243,890 is not evenly divisible by 4 because the number made by its last two digits (90) is not evenly divisible by 4. 243,890 is evenly divisible by 5 because its unit's digits (0) is a 0 or a 5. 243,890 is not evenly divisible by 6 because it is not evenly divisible by both 2 and 3. 243,890 is not evenly divisible by 9 because the sum

of its digits (26) is not evenly divisible by 9. 243,890 is evenly divisible by 10 because its unit's digit is a 0.

7. [2] 7,442 is evenly divisible by 2 because its unit's digit (2) is evenly divisible by 2. 7,442 is not evenly divisible by 3 because the sum of its digits (17) is not evenly divisible by 3. 7,442 is not evenly divisible by 4 because the number made by its last two digits (42) is not evenly divisible by 4. 7,442 is not evenly divisible by 5 because its unit's digits (2) is not a 0 or a 5. 7,442 is not evenly divisible by 6 because it is not evenly divisible by both 2 and 3. 7,442 is not evenly divisible by 9 because the sum of its digits (17) is not evenly divisible by 9. 7,442 is not evenly divisible by 10 because its unit's digit is not a 0.

8. [3, 9] 19,683 is not evenly divisible by 2 because its unit's digit (3) is not evenly divisible by 2. 19,683 is evenly divisible by 3 because the sum of its digits (27) is evenly divisible by 3. 19,683 is not evenly divisible by 4 because the number made by its last two digits (83) is not evenly divisible by 4. 19,683 is not evenly divisible by 5 because its unit's digits (3) is not a 0 or a 5. 19,683 is not evenly divisible by 6 because it is not evenly divisible by both 2 and 3. 19,683 is evenly divisible by 9 because the sum of its digits (27) is evenly divisible by 9. 19,683 is not evenly divisible by 10 because its unit's digit (1) is not a 0.

9. [2, 4] 1,048,576 is evenly divisible by 2 because its unit's digit (6) is evenly divisible by 2. 1,048,576 is not evenly divisible by 3 because the sum of its digits (31) is not evenly divisible by 3. 1,048,576 is evenly divisible by 4 because the number made by its last two digits (76) is evenly divisible by 4. 1,048,576 is not evenly divisible by 5 because its unit's digits (6) is not a 0 or a 5. 1,048,576 is not evenly divisible by 6 because it is not evenly divisible by both 2 and 3. 1,048,576 is not evenly divisible by 9 because the sum of its digits (31) is not evenly divisible by 9. 1,048,576 is not evenly divisible by 10 because its unit's digit is not a 0.

10. [2, 3, 4, 5, 6, 9, 10] 1,555,200 is evenly divisible by 2 because its unit's digit (0) is evenly divisible by 2. 1,555,200 is evenly divisible by 3 because the sum of its digits (18) is evenly divisible by 3. 1,555,200 is evenly divisible by 4 because the number made by its last two digits (0) is evenly divisible by 4. 1,555,200 is evenly divisible by 5 because its unit's digits (0) is a 0 or a 5. 1,555,200 is evenly divisible by 6 because it is evenly divisible by both 2 and 3. 1,555,200 is evenly divisible by 9 because the sum of its digits (18) is evenly divisible by 9. 1,555,200 is evenly divisible by 10 because its unit's digit is a 0.

Fractions

Fraction Parts and Types

Fractions are made up of two numbers separated by a fraction *bar*. The number on top of the bar is called the *numerator*, while the number below it is called the *denominator*. Fractions are used to show the *relationship* of a part to a whole (if Piglet ate 4 pieces of Pooh's pie of 6 equal slices, Piglet ate $\frac{4}{6}$ or $\frac{2}{3}$ of the pie), *division* of one number by another number ($1 \div 2$ can be expressed $\frac{1}{2}$), or a *ratio* of two quantities (the ratio of pears to peaches in Grandmother's basket is 1:3; that is, there is 1 pear for every 3 peaches in the basket).

Fractions can be either *proper*, such as $\frac{7}{9}$ or *improper*, such as $\frac{9}{7}$. In proper fractions, the numerator is smaller than the denominator. In improper fractions, the numerator is either the same size as the denominator, or larger. A whole number, together with a fraction, is a *mixed number*. $1\frac{2}{7}$ is a mixed number.

Equivalent Fractions and Conversions

Because the value of a number does not change when that number is multiplied or divided by 1, fractions can be either raised or reduced, respectively, through the multiplication (to raise) or the division (to reduce) of *both* the numerator and the denominator by the *same* non-zero number. (Any non-zero number over itself equals 1.)

Most fractions you will be dealing with will be proper fractions, reduced to their lowest terms. $\frac{7}{9}$ is such a fraction. It is proper, and it cannot be reduced; that is, reduction by evenly dividing both the numerator and the denominator by the same number greater than 1 is *not* possible. Suppose, though, that you are faced with the fraction $\frac{28}{36}$. Even division of both the numerator and the denominator by 4 is possible, and results in a fraction equivalent to $\frac{28}{36}$, but one lower in terms, and hence easier to work with. $\frac{7}{9}$ and $\frac{28}{36}$ are called *equivalent* fractions, because they have the *same* value. $\frac{7}{9}$ is $\frac{28}{36}$ reduced to its lowest terms and $\frac{28}{36}$ is $\frac{7}{9}$ raised to a higher term.

Improper fractions can be changed to their mixed number equivalents. This is done by *dividing* the numerator of the fraction by the denominator (recall that one of the things fractions represent is division). 9 divided by 7 equals 1 with a remainder of 2. You'd write the quotient as a whole number and the remainder as the numerator on top of the original denominator ($1\frac{2}{7}$). Another way to think about this is to recognize that $\frac{9}{7}$ is equal to $\frac{7}{7}+\frac{2}{7}$, or $1\frac{2}{7}$. The mixed number $1\frac{2}{7}$ could be changed back into an improper fraction by multiplying the denominator of the fraction, 7, by the whole number, 1. The result, 7, is then added to the numerator of the fraction, 2, and put on top of the original denominator. Whole numbers, too, can be converted to mixed numbers. This is done by putting the whole number over a denominator of 1. $8 = \frac{8}{1}$, for instance and $121 = \frac{121}{1}$.

PRACTICE SET 5

Reduce the following fractions:

1. $\dfrac{4}{8}$

2. $\dfrac{9}{12}$

3. $\dfrac{15}{27}$

4. $\dfrac{58}{102}$

5. $\dfrac{180}{120}$

Convert the following improper fractions to mixed form:

6. $\dfrac{3}{2}$

7. $\dfrac{10}{7}$

8. $\dfrac{26}{3}$

9. $\frac{16}{15}$

10. $\frac{15}{5}$

Convert from mixed form to improper fractions:

11. $1\frac{2}{3}$

12. $8\frac{1}{2}$

13. $10\frac{3}{4}$

14. $21\frac{1}{4}$

15. $1\frac{1}{100}$

Are these equivalent fractions?

16. $\frac{2}{7}$ $\frac{8}{28}$

17. $\frac{3}{2}$ $\frac{39}{29}$

18. $\dfrac{5}{6}$ $\quad$ $\dfrac{390}{468}$

19. $\dfrac{7}{5}$ $\quad$ $\dfrac{35}{25}$

20. $\dfrac{4}{5}$ $\quad$ $\dfrac{16}{25}$

ANSWERS—PRACTICE SET 5

1. $\frac{1}{2}$

2. $\frac{3}{4}$

3. $\frac{5}{9}$

4. $\frac{29}{51}$

5. $\frac{3}{2}$

6. $1\frac{1}{2}$

7. $1\frac{3}{7}$

8. $8\frac{2}{3}$

9. $1\frac{1}{15}$

10. 3

11. $\frac{5}{3}$

12. $\frac{17}{2}$

13. $\frac{43}{4}$

14. $\frac{85}{4}$

15. $\frac{101}{100}$

16. yes $\frac{8}{28} \div \frac{4}{4} = \frac{2}{7}$

17. no, 29 is prime, so the fraction $\frac{39}{29}$ can't be reduced

18. yes $\dfrac{390}{468} \div \dfrac{78}{78} = \dfrac{5}{6}$

19. yes $\dfrac{35}{25} \div \dfrac{5}{5} = \dfrac{7}{5}$

20. no $\dfrac{16}{25}$ does not reduce

Adding and Subtracting Fractions

To add or subtract *like* fractions (fractions that have the same denominator):

(1) add or subtract the numerators
(2) put the result over the denominator

$\frac{3}{4} + \frac{2}{4} = \frac{5}{4}$ and $\frac{11}{10} - \frac{2}{10} = \frac{9}{10}$. It is often useful to reduce the end product to its lowest terms, if applicable. $\frac{30}{40} - \frac{20}{40} = \frac{10}{40} = \frac{1}{4}$ and $\frac{16}{32} + \frac{12}{32} = \frac{28}{32} = \frac{7}{8}$.

To add or subtract *unlike* fractions:

(1) find a common denominator and rewrite the fractions as equivalents with the common denominator
(2) add or subtract the numerators
(3) put the result over the common denominator

Finding a common denominator involves finding a common multiple of the denominators. Multiplying the denominators is a reliable method of finding a common denominator, but oftentimes simply multiplying one of the fractions by a certain equivalent of 1 will set the denominators equal. Such is the case in Sample Question 6:

Sample Question 6: $\dfrac{22}{121} + \dfrac{31}{11} =$

Process (words)	Process (numbers)
(1) find a common denominator	(1) $\dfrac{22}{121} = \dfrac{22}{121}$
	$\dfrac{31}{11} \times \dfrac{11}{11} = \dfrac{341}{121}$ $\left(\text{note that } \dfrac{11}{11} = 1\right)$
(2) add the numerators	(2) $22 + 341 = 363$
(3) put the result over the common denominator	(3) $\dfrac{363}{121}$
(4) reduce and/or simplify	(4) $\dfrac{363}{121} = 3$

In Sample Question 7, the method of multiplying the denominators is used:

Sample Question 7: $\dfrac{5}{10} + \dfrac{6}{7} =$

Process (words)	Process (numbers)
(1) find a common denominator	(1) $\dfrac{5}{10} \times \dfrac{7}{7} = \dfrac{35}{70}$ $\dfrac{6}{7} \times \dfrac{10}{10} = \dfrac{60}{70}$
(2) add the numerators	(2) $35 + 60 = 95$
(3) put the result over the common denominator	(3) $\dfrac{95}{70}$
(4) reduce and/or simplify	(4) $\dfrac{95}{70} = \dfrac{70}{70} + \dfrac{25}{70} = 1\dfrac{25}{70} = 1\dfrac{5}{14}$

When multiplying the denominators to find a common denominator, an easy way to find the numerators is to cross multiply the original fractions, from lower right to upper left, and from lower left to upper right. Using this method for the above problem, you would quickly end up with 35 and 60 as your numerators ($7 \times 5 = 35$ and $10 \times 6 = 60$).

In general, multiplying the denominators to find a common denominator yields large and hard to manage numbers. When adding or subtracting large unlike fractions, you will probably want to find the smallest common denominator, otherwise known as the *least common denominator*. The least common denominator is simply the least common multiple of the denominators.

To find the least common multiple of two or more denominators:

(1) prime factor each denominator
(2) circle all the factors of the first denominator
(3) eliminate repeating factors in the other denominators
(4) multiply the circled factors

Once the least common denominator has been found, the numerators must be brought up to par. Multiply each numerator by the number that raises its respective denominator to the least common denominator. (This number can be arrived at by dividing the least common denominator by the old, original denominator.) The new like fractions, being equivalent to the originals, are now ready to be added or subtracted as is indicated. Suppose you were asked to add $\frac{4}{12} + \frac{3}{14} + \frac{7}{18}$. Obviously, multiplying $12 \times 14 \times 18$ would yield a very large common denominator (in fact it's 3,024). In Sample Question 8, the least common denominator method is used:

Sample Question 8: $\dfrac{4}{12} + \dfrac{3}{14} + \dfrac{7}{18} =$

Process (words)	Process (numbers)

(1) find the LCD

(1) $12 = 2 \times 2 \times 3$
$14 = 2 \times 7$
$18 = 2 \times 3 \times 3$
$LCD = 2 \times 2 \times 3 \times 3 \times 7$
$LCD = 252$

(2) determine the numerators

(2) $252 \div 12 = 21 \qquad 4 \times 21 = 84$
$252 \div 14 = 18 \qquad 3 \times 18 = 54$
$252 \div 18 = 14 \qquad 7 \times 14 = 98$

(3) add the numerators

(3) $84 + 54 + 98 = 236$

(4) put the result over the LCD

(4) $\dfrac{236}{252}$

(5) reduce and/or simplify

(5) $\dfrac{59}{63}$

PRACTICE SET 6

Solve the following equations and express the answers in reduced form.

1. $\dfrac{2}{3} + \dfrac{2}{3} =$

2. $\dfrac{5}{12} + \dfrac{3}{12} =$

3. $\dfrac{1}{2} - \dfrac{1}{3} =$

4. $\dfrac{6}{7} + \dfrac{7}{8} =$

5. $\dfrac{241}{356} - \dfrac{241}{356} =$

6. $\dfrac{2}{3} + \dfrac{1}{4} =$

7. $\dfrac{3}{5} - \dfrac{11}{125} =$

8. $\dfrac{7}{13} + \dfrac{3}{17} =$

9. $\dfrac{1}{2} + \dfrac{1}{3} + \dfrac{1}{4} =$

10. $\dfrac{2}{3} - \dfrac{1}{4} + \dfrac{7}{9} =$

ANSWERS AND EXPLANATIONS—PRACTICE SET 6

1. $\dfrac{2}{3}+\dfrac{2}{3}=\dfrac{4}{3}$

2. $\dfrac{5}{12}+\dfrac{3}{12}=\dfrac{8}{12}=\dfrac{2}{3}$

3. $\dfrac{1}{2}-\dfrac{1}{3}=\dfrac{3}{6}-\dfrac{2}{6}=\dfrac{1}{6}$

4. $\dfrac{6}{7}+\dfrac{7}{8}=\dfrac{48}{56}+\dfrac{49}{56}=\dfrac{97}{56}$

5. $\dfrac{241}{356}-\dfrac{241}{356}=0$

6. $\dfrac{2}{3}+\dfrac{1}{4}=\dfrac{8}{12}+\dfrac{3}{12}=\dfrac{11}{12}$

7. $\dfrac{3}{5}-\dfrac{11}{125}=\dfrac{75}{125}-\dfrac{11}{125}=\dfrac{64}{125}$

8. $\dfrac{7}{13}+\dfrac{3}{17}=\dfrac{119}{221}+\dfrac{39}{221}=\dfrac{158}{221}$

9. $\dfrac{1}{2}+\dfrac{1}{3}+\dfrac{1}{4}=\dfrac{6}{12}+\dfrac{4}{12}+\dfrac{3}{12}=\dfrac{13}{12}$

10. $\dfrac{2}{3}-\dfrac{1}{4}+\dfrac{7}{9}=\dfrac{24}{36}-\dfrac{9}{36}+\dfrac{28}{36}=\dfrac{43}{36}$

Multiplying and Dividing Fractions

Multiplying fractions is straightforward. Simply multiply across the numerators to find the end numerator and across the denominators to find the end denominator. When possible, reduce the fractions by cross and/or vertical canceling before multiplying.

Sample Question 9: Multiply $\dfrac{8}{18}\times\dfrac{6}{20}\times\dfrac{14}{3}\times\dfrac{2}{4}$

Process (words)	Process (numbers)
(1) reduce through cross and vertical canceling	(1) $\dfrac{2\cancel{8}}{3\cancel{18}}\times\dfrac{1\cancel{6}}{5\cancel{20}}\times\dfrac{\cancel{14}^{7}}{3}\times\dfrac{2}{\cancel{4}\cancel{2}_{1}}^{1}$
(2) multiply the numerators	(2) $2\times1\times7=14$

(3) multiply the denominators   (3) $3 \times 5 \times 3 = 45$

(4) put the numerator product over the   (4) $\dfrac{14}{45}$
    denominator product

Dividing fractions is also straightforward. First flip the divisor (the second fraction) and then multiply. Here, you will want to reduce *after* flipping, but *before* multiplying.

Sample Question 10: $\dfrac{9}{18} \div \dfrac{2}{100}$

<u>Process (words)</u>	<u>Process (numbers)</u>
(1) flip the divisor	(1) $\dfrac{9}{18} \times \dfrac{100}{2}$
(2) reduce through cross and vertical canceling	(2) $\dfrac{{}^{1}\cancel{9}}{{}_{2}\cancel{18}} \times \dfrac{\cancel{100}^{\,50}}{\cancel{2}_{\,1}}$
(3) multiply the numerators	(3) $1 \times 50 = 50$
(4) multiply the denominators	(4) $2 \times 1 = 2$
(5) put the numerator product over the denominator product	(5) $\dfrac{50}{2}$
(6) reduce	(6) 25

Complex Fractions

Occasionally, you will encounter a fraction whose numerator or denominator or both are fractions. There are two ways to deal with these *complex* fractions:

1. Multiply each term in the complex fraction by a common multiple of all of the denominators, preferably, the least common multiple, thus eliminating the denominators, and then complete the operations.

$$\frac{\frac{1}{2}+\frac{2}{5}}{\frac{3}{8}+\frac{18}{10}-\frac{6}{3}} = \frac{120\left[\frac{1}{2}+\frac{2}{5}\right]}{120\left[\frac{3}{8}+\frac{18}{10}-\frac{6}{3}\right]}$$

$$= \frac{60+48}{45+216-240}$$

$$= \frac{108}{21}$$

$$= \frac{36}{7}$$

$$= 5\frac{1}{7}$$

2. Another approach is to complete the operations (combine the numbers, etc.) in the numerator and the denominator separately, and then divide the top fraction by the bottom fraction by flipping the bottom fraction and multiplying.

$$\frac{\frac{1}{2}+\frac{2}{5}}{\frac{3}{8}+\frac{18}{10}-\frac{6}{3}}$$

$$\frac{1}{2}+\frac{2}{5} = \frac{5}{10}+\frac{4}{10} = \frac{9}{10}$$

and

$$\frac{3}{8}+\frac{18}{10}-\frac{6}{3} = \frac{45}{120}+\frac{216}{120}-\frac{240}{120} = \frac{21}{120}$$

$$\frac{\frac{9}{10}}{\frac{21}{120}} = \frac{9}{10} \div \frac{21}{120} = \frac{9}{1\cancel{10}} \times \frac{\cancel{120}^{12}}{21} = \frac{108}{21} = \frac{36}{7} = 5\frac{1}{7}$$

PRACTICE SET 7

1. $\dfrac{1}{2} \times \dfrac{1}{3} =$

2. $\dfrac{1}{2} \div \dfrac{1}{3} =$

3. $\dfrac{7}{2} \times \dfrac{5}{14} =$

4. $\dfrac{7}{8} \div \dfrac{7}{8} =$

5. $\dfrac{7}{8} \div \dfrac{8}{7} =$

6. $\dfrac{2}{3} \times \dfrac{3}{2} =$

7. $\dfrac{\frac{3}{8}}{\frac{1}{4}} =$

8. $\dfrac{\frac{1}{2} + \frac{1}{3}}{\frac{1}{2} + \frac{2}{3}} =$

9. $\dfrac{\frac{2}{5} + \frac{1}{7}}{\frac{1}{10} + \frac{1}{8}} =$

ANSWERS AND EXPLANATIONS—PRACTICE SET 7

1. $\dfrac{1}{2} \times \dfrac{1}{3} = \dfrac{1}{6}$

2. $\dfrac{1}{2} \div \dfrac{1}{3} = \dfrac{1}{2} \times \dfrac{3}{1} = \dfrac{3}{2}$

3. $\dfrac{{}^{1}7}{2} \times \dfrac{5}{14_{2}} = \dfrac{5}{4}$

4. $\dfrac{7}{8} \div \dfrac{7}{8} = 1$

5. $\dfrac{7}{8} \div \dfrac{8}{7} = \dfrac{7}{8} \times \dfrac{7}{8} = \dfrac{49}{64}$

6. $\dfrac{2}{3} \times \dfrac{3}{2} = \dfrac{6}{6} = 1$

7. $\dfrac{\frac{3}{8}}{\frac{1}{4}} = \dfrac{3}{8} \div \dfrac{1}{4} = \dfrac{3}{{}_{2}8} \times \dfrac{{}^{1}\cancel{4}}{1} = \dfrac{3}{2}$

8. $\dfrac{\frac{1}{2}+\frac{1}{3}}{\frac{1}{2}+\frac{2}{3}} = \dfrac{6\left(\frac{1}{2}+\frac{1}{3}\right)}{6\left(\frac{1}{2}+\frac{2}{3}\right)} = \dfrac{3+2}{3+4} = \dfrac{5}{7}$

9. $\dfrac{\frac{2}{5}+\frac{1}{7}}{\frac{1}{10}+\frac{1}{8}} = \dfrac{\frac{14}{35}+\frac{5}{35}}{\frac{4}{40}+\frac{5}{40}} = \dfrac{\frac{19}{35}}{\frac{9}{40}} = \dfrac{19}{{}_{7}\cancel{35}} \times \dfrac{\cancel{40}^{8}}{9} = \dfrac{152}{63}$

Comparing Fractions

Positive fractions can be compared in a number of different ways:

1. *Cross multiply* the denominator of each fraction by the numerator of the other and compare the products. *Always* cross multiply from the bottom up (as if making a special X, in which both strokes start at the bottom), and mark the product where you end up, then compare the two numbers. If the number on the right is greater, the fraction on the right is greater, and vice versa.

$$ ^{(28)}\ \dfrac{4}{5} \diagdown\!\!\!\!\diagup \dfrac{6}{7}\ ^{(30)} $$

2. Sometimes, you can eyeball it. Suppose you are comparing $\frac{9}{20}$ to $\frac{26}{50}$. The later is slightly greater than $\frac{1}{2}$, the former is slightly less than $\frac{1}{2}$. $\frac{26}{50}$ is thus the greater fraction.

3. If the denominators are the same, compare the numerators. The fraction with the larger numerator is greater. $\frac{2}{5}$ is greater than $\frac{1}{5}$ and $\frac{1}{2}$ is less than $\frac{3}{4}$ $\left(\frac{1}{2}=\frac{2}{4}\right)$.

4. If the numerators are the same, compare the denominators. The fraction with the smaller denominator is greater. $\frac{1}{3}$ of the pie is more than $\frac{1}{4}$ of the pie. If two equal size pizzas are cut up, one into 6 even slices and the other into 8 even slices, and you could have 3 slices from either, which would you choose, $\frac{3}{6}$ of the first pizza or $\frac{3}{8}$ of the second?

Most would choose the three larger pieces, or $\frac{1}{2}$ of the first pizza.

If you're comparing more than two fractions, compare the first two, keep the greater fraction and compare it with the third and so on.

Sample Question 11: Which is greatest: $\dfrac{3}{10}$ or $\dfrac{4}{8}$ or $\dfrac{6}{7}$ or $\dfrac{4}{7}$

Process (words)	Process (numbers)		
(1) compare the first two fractions (eyeball)	(1) $\dfrac{3}{10}$	$\dfrac{4}{8}$	$\left(\dfrac{4}{8} \text{ is } \dfrac{1}{2}\right)$
(2) compare the greater with the third (eyeball)	(2) $\dfrac{4}{8}$	$\dfrac{6}{7}$	$\left(\dfrac{6}{7} \text{ is more than } \dfrac{1}{2}\right)$
(3) compare the greater with the fourth (compare numerators)	(3) $\dfrac{6}{7}$	$\dfrac{4}{7}$	(6 is greater)

42

PRACTICE SET 8

Which fraction is largest?

	A	B	C
1.	$\dfrac{3}{8}$	$\dfrac{4}{8}$	
2.	$\dfrac{7}{10}$	$\dfrac{4}{5}$	
3.	$\dfrac{16}{30}$	$\dfrac{74}{150}$	
4.	$\dfrac{12}{32}$	$\dfrac{9}{16}$	
5.	$\dfrac{5}{4}$	$\dfrac{62}{63}$	
6.	$\dfrac{1}{11}$	$\dfrac{1}{9}$	
7.	$\dfrac{24}{100}$	$\dfrac{21}{80}$	
8.	$\dfrac{7}{8}$	$\dfrac{8}{9}$	

	A	B	C
9.	$\frac{1}{2}$	$\frac{34}{70}$	$\frac{88}{180}$
10.	$\frac{32}{100}$	$\frac{66}{200}$	$\frac{9}{24}$

44

ANSWERS AND EXPLANATIONS—PRACTICE SET 8

1. B $\frac{4}{8}$ is larger. The denominators are the same, so the fraction with the larger numerator is greater.

2. B $\frac{4}{5}$ is larger: $\overset{35}{\frac{7}{10}} \diagup\!\!\!\!\!\diagdown \overset{40}{\frac{4}{5}}$

3. A $\frac{16}{30}$ is larger: $\overset{2400}{\frac{16}{30}} \diagup\!\!\!\!\!\diagdown \frac{74}{150}{}^{2200}$

4. B $\frac{9}{16}$ is larger: $\overset{6}{\underset{16}{\cancel{\frac{12}{32}}}}\quad \frac{9}{16}$

5. A $\frac{5}{4}$ is larger: $\frac{5}{4}$ is larger than 1, and so is larger than $\frac{62}{63}$.

6. B $\frac{1}{9}$ is larger: The numerators are the same, so the fraction with the smaller denominator is greater.

7. B $\frac{21}{80}$ is larger: $\frac{21}{80}$ is just over $\frac{1}{4}$, whereas $\frac{24}{100}$ is just under $\frac{1}{4}$.

8. B $\frac{8}{9}$ is larger: $\overset{63}{\frac{7}{8}} \diagup\!\!\!\!\!\diagdown \overset{64}{\frac{8}{9}}$

9. A $\frac{1}{2}$ is largest. $\frac{34}{70}$ and $\frac{88}{180}$ are both just under $\frac{1}{2}$.

10. C $\frac{9}{24}$ is largest: $\frac{66}{200}=\frac{33}{100}$ and: $\overset{792}{\frac{33}{100}} \diagup\!\!\!\!\!\diagdown \frac{9}{24}{}^{900}$

Decimals

Interpreting Decimals as Fractions

A decimal consists of a *whole number*, which is to the left of the *decimal point,* plus a *decimal fraction*, which is to the right. In 5.25, 5 is the whole number part of the decimal and .25 is the decimal fraction part. Decimal fractions represent common fractions. The decimal fraction .25, for instance, represents the common fraction $\frac{25}{100}$ or $\frac{1}{4}$. So 5.25 is the same thing as the mixed number $5\frac{1}{4}$.

Where did the denominator of 100 come from? Since decimals are used to express dollars and cents, think of the 5.25 as 5 dollars and 25 cents. What part is 25 cents, or a quarter, of a dollar? 100 pennies make a dollar, as do 4 quarters. 25 cents, then, is $\frac{25}{100}$ of a dollar, or $\frac{1}{4}$. Not all decimals look like sums of money, though, so there must be another method of determining just what common fraction a decimal fraction represents.

Intuitively, you probably recognize that $\frac{5}{10}$ is ten times greater than $\frac{5}{100}$, which is in turn ten times greater than $\frac{5}{1000}$; and that .5 is ten times greater than .05, which is in turn ten times greater than .005. These relationships demonstrate a fundamental principle regarding the significance of place on value (one very much related to the value of different numbers in a decimal fraction): each place in a number is worth ten times more than the place to its immediate right. That is *why* .5 is ten times more than .05, and ten times less than 5. Number places are named according to the value they afford the numeral in them:

thousands, hundreds, tens, units . tenths, hundredths, thousandths

The number 6,322.683 can be expressed in word form, mixed number form and decimal form:

1. 6 thousands + 3 hundreds + 2 tens + 2 units + 6 tenths + 8 hundredths + 3 thousandths

2. $6 \times 1000 + 3 \times 100 + 2 \times 10 + 2 + 1 + \dfrac{6}{10} + \dfrac{8}{100} + \dfrac{3}{1000}$

3. $6000 + 300 + 20 + 2 + .6 + .08 + .003$

An understanding of the place value concept makes sense of the general rules for converting *decimals* to *fractions.*

To change a decimal fraction to a common fraction:

(1) put the *actual* numbers that make up the decimal fraction in the numerator
(2) put a 1 plus as many zeros as there are numerals in the decimal fraction in the denominator

A consideration: Zeros to the far right of a decimal fraction do not effect the *value* of a decimal fraction, but do effect conversions. For instance 5.25 = 5.2500, but $5\frac{25}{100}$ does not equal

$5\frac{2,500}{100}$. When converting decimal fractions with a zero or several zeros to the far right, you either must eliminate the zeros before the conversion, or apply them consistently. For instance, if you were converting .2500 to a common fraction, and you decided to keep the zeros, you would end up with a denominator of 10,000 (there are 4 numerals to the right of the decimal), and a numerator of 2500. The whole fraction would be $\frac{2,500}{10,000}$ which reduces to $\frac{25}{100}$. (Eliminating the zeros from the beginning would give you $\frac{25}{100}$ straight away.)

Interpreting Fractions as Decimals

Fractions whose denominators are multiples of ten can be converted to decimals by employing a reverse of the above. $\frac{25}{100}$ thus becomes .25 because there are two zeros after the 1 in the denominator, and the numerator is 25. These and other kinds of fractions can be converted in another way; namely, by dividing the numerator by the denominator:

$$\frac{5}{10} = .5 \quad \text{or} \quad 10\overline{)\begin{array}{r} .5 \\ 5.0 \\ \underline{5.0} \\ 0.0 \end{array}}$$

$$\frac{5}{100} = .05 \quad \text{or} \quad 100\overline{)\begin{array}{r} .05 \\ 5.00 \\ \underline{5.00} \\ 0.00 \end{array}}$$

$$\frac{5}{1000} = .005 \quad \text{or} \quad 1000\overline{)\begin{array}{r} .005 \\ 5.000 \\ \underline{5.000} \\ 0.000 \end{array}}$$

PRACTICE SET 9

Express the following fractions as decimals:

1. $\dfrac{1}{10}$

2. $\dfrac{1}{8}$

3. $\dfrac{1}{5}$

4. $\dfrac{1}{4}$

5. $\dfrac{1}{3}$

6. $\dfrac{1}{2}$

7. $\dfrac{3}{4}$

8. $\dfrac{13}{20}$

9. $\dfrac{32}{25}$

10. $\dfrac{125}{50}$

Express the following decimals as fractions:

11. 0.5

12. 2.1

13. 0.625

14. 0.666...

15. 0.211

ANSWERS AND EXPLANATIONS—PRACTICE SET 9

1. 0.1

```
       .1
   10)1.0
      1 0
        0
```

2. 0.125

```
       .125
    8)1.000
      8
      20
      16
       40
       40
        0
```

3. 0.2

```
      .2
   5)1.0
     1.0
       0
```

4. 0.25

```
      .25
   4)1.00
     8
     20
     20
      0
```

5. 0.333...

```
      .333...
   3)1.000
     9
     10
      9
      10
       9
       1
```

6. 0.5

```
      .5
  2)1.0
    1 0
    ___
       0
```

7. 0.75

```
      .75
  4)3.00
    28
    ___
    20
    20
    ___
     0
```

8. 0.65

```
        .65
  20)13.00
     120
     ____
     100
     100
     ____
       0
```

9. 1.28

```
       1.28
  25)32.00
     25
     ___
     70
     50
     ___
     200
     200
     ____
       0
```

10. 2.5

```
        2.5
  50)125.0
     100
     ____
     250
     250
     ____
       0
```

11. $\frac{1}{2}$

$$0.5 = \frac{5}{10} = \frac{1}{2}$$

12. $\dfrac{21}{10}$ or $2\dfrac{1}{10}$

$$2.1 = 2\dfrac{1}{10} = \dfrac{21}{10}$$

13. $\dfrac{5}{8}$

$$0.625 = \dfrac{625}{1000} = \dfrac{25}{40} = \dfrac{5}{8}$$

14. $\dfrac{2}{3}$

Decimal equivalent of frequently appearing fraction (see page 58).

15. $\dfrac{211}{1000}$

$$0.211 = \dfrac{211}{1000}$$

Rounding Off Decimals

It's often useful to round off unwieldy decimals to the nearest tenth, or maybe hundredth. To do so simply underline the numeral in the place you are rounding off to (it's the numeral that *may* change) and look to the numeral to its right. If that numeral is 5 or more round the underlined numeral up one and drop the numerals to the right. If that numeral is less than 5 leave the underlined numeral as is and drop the numerals to the right. Rounding 12.345 to the nearest tenth would leave you with 12.3. Rounding 12.345 to the nearest hundredth would leave you with 12.35.

Adding and Subtracting Decimals

To add or subtract decimals, stack them vertically, with the decimal points in alignment, and add or subtract as you would whole numbers. (Treat empty spaces as zeros and bring the decimal straight down into the result.)

Sample Question 12: Add 3.222 + 9.05 + 16.030 + 65

Process (words)	Process (numbers)

(1) align the numbers vertically	(1) 3.222
	     9.050
	   16.030
	   65.000

(2) add as you would whole numbers	(2) 93.302

Multiplying Decimals

Multiplying decimals is just like multiplying whole numbers except that you must figure out where to place the decimal point in the product. This is done by counting the total number of numerals in the decimal fractions of each of the numbers you've multiplied (all numerals to the right of the decimal points), and placing the decimal point in the product so that the number of numerals in the decimal fraction of the product equal that number. Here are some examples:

$25 \times .25 = 6.25$

$62 \times .003 = .186$

$920 \times .0004 = .368$

$.3 \times .2 \times .8 \times .06 = .00288$

Dividing Decimals

Dividing decimals is just like dividing whole numbers except that you must first convert the divisor into a whole number. This is done by moving the decimal point of the divisor all the way to the right and then moving the decimal point of the dividend the exact same number of places to the right. You may need to add zeros onto the end of the dividend. Recall that zeros to the far right of a decimal fraction do not change the value of the decimal fraction. Oftentimes, your division will go on and on and you will want to stop and round off the quotient. Here are some examples:

Example 1:

$.45 \div .3$

$$
\begin{array}{r}
1.5 \\
3\,\overline{)4.5} \\
\underline{3} \\
15 \\
\underline{15} \\
0
\end{array}
$$
← (movement one place to the right makes our divisor whole)

Example 2:

$2.670 \div .089$

$$
\begin{array}{r}
30. \\
89\,\overline{)2670.} \\
\underline{2670} \\
00 \\
\underline{0} \\
0
\end{array}
$$
← (movement three places to the right makes our divisor whole)

54

Example 3:

.4960 ÷ 1.55

$$\begin{array}{r} .32 \\ 155. \overline{)49.60} \\ \underline{4650} \\ 310 \\ \underline{310} \\ 0 \end{array}$$ ← (movement two places to the right makes our divisor whole)

PRACTICE SET 10

Round the following numbers to two decimal places:

1. 12.169

2. 4.164

3. 10.23579

4. 10.23479

5. 0.009

Perform operations:

6. $1.1 + 1.2 =$

7. $3.12 - 2.06 =$

8. $9.99 + .01 =$

9. $16 + 4.25 + 250.006 =$

10. $0.1 \times 10 =$

11. $0.25 \times 16 =$

12. $0.56 \times 3.01 =$

13. $12.06 \times 1.73 =$

14. $20,000 \times 0.0005 =$

ANSWERS AND EXPLANATIONS—PRACTICE SET 10

1. 12.17
2. 4.16
3. 10.24
4. 10.23
5. 0.01

6. 2.3

$$
\begin{array}{r}
1.1 \\
+1.2 \\
\hline
2.3
\end{array}
$$

7. 1.06

$$
\begin{array}{r}
3.12 \\
-2.06 \\
\hline
1.06
\end{array}
$$

8. 10

$$
\begin{array}{r}
9.99 \\
+.01 \\
\hline
10.00
\end{array}
$$

9. 270.256

$$
\begin{array}{r}
16.0 \\
4.25 \\
+250.006 \\
\hline
270.256
\end{array}
$$

10. 1

$$
\begin{array}{r}
0.1 \\
\times 10 \\
\hline
00 \\
010 \\
\hline
1.0
\end{array}
$$

11. 4

$$
\begin{array}{r}
0.25 \\
\times 16 \\
\hline
150 \\
250 \\
\hline
4.00
\end{array}
$$

12. 1.6856

$$
\begin{array}{r}
0.56 \\
\times\,3.01 \\
\hline
56 \\
0000 \\
16800 \\
\hline
1.6856
\end{array}
$$

13. 20.8638

$$
\begin{array}{r}
12.06 \\
\times\,1.73 \\
\hline
3618 \\
84420 \\
120600 \\
\hline
20.8638
\end{array}
$$

14. 10

$$
\begin{array}{r}
20,000 \\
\times\,0.0005 \\
\hline
10.0000
\end{array}
$$

Comparing Decimals

To compare decimal fractions stack them vertically, with the decimal points in alignment, and fill in zeros to the far right of the fractions which are shorter than the longest fraction[s] until each fraction is of equal length. (This gives each decimal fraction the same denominator.) Then compare the numbers in the decimal fractions (the numerators).

Example: Which is greatest .234 or .00999 or .059 or .22222?

<u>Process (words)</u>   <u>Process (numbers)</u>

(1) align the numbers vertically   (1) .23400 $\dfrac{23,400}{100,000}$

                                                       .00999 $\dfrac{999}{100,000}$

                                                       .05900 $\dfrac{5,900}{100,000}$

                                                       .22222 $\dfrac{22,222}{100,000}$

(2) determine relative values   (2) .23400 is greatest

58

Here are the decimal equivalents of some frequently appearing fractions:

$\frac{1}{2} = .5$

$\frac{1}{8} = .125$

$\frac{1}{3} = .333...$

$\frac{2}{3} = .666...$

$\frac{1}{4} = .25$

$\frac{3}{4} = .75$

$\frac{1}{5} = .2$

$\frac{2}{5} = .4$

$\frac{3}{5} = .6$

$\frac{4}{5} = .8$

PRACTICE SET 11

Which is greater?

1. .925 or 1.025

2. .0365 or .008365

3. .1856 or 18.56

4. .00009 or .000009

5. 100.002 or 99.9999

Which is lesser?

6. .065 or $\frac{4}{5}$

7. $\dfrac{8}{5}$ or 8.5

8. .325 or $\dfrac{1}{5}$

9. $\dfrac{7}{8}$ or 1.378

10. $\dfrac{1}{3}$ or .666

What is the decimal equivalent of these common fractions?

11. $\dfrac{2}{3}$

12. $\dfrac{1}{2}$

13. $\dfrac{2}{5}$

14. $\dfrac{1}{5}$

15. $\dfrac{4}{5}$

ANSWERS AND EXPLANATIONS—PRACTICE SET 11

1. 1.025
2. .0365
3. 18.56
4. .00009
5. 100.002

6. .065   .065 is less than $\frac{1}{10}$ and so is less than $\frac{4}{5}$.

7. $\frac{8}{5}$ $\frac{8}{5}$ is less than $\frac{10}{5}$ or 2, and so is less than 8.5.

8. $\frac{1}{3}$ .325 = $\frac{325}{1000}$ which is over $\frac{250}{1000}$ or $\frac{1}{4}$, and so is greater than $\frac{1}{5}$.

9. $\frac{7}{8}$ $\frac{7}{8}$ is less than 1 and so is less than 1.378.

10. $\frac{1}{3}$ $\frac{1}{3}$ is less than $\frac{1}{2}$ or .5, and so is less than .666.

11. .666
12. .5
13. .4
14. .2
15. .8

Percents

Reading Percents

Cent, from the Latin word *centum*, means "100." Per means "for each." *Percent*, then, quite literally means "for each 100." If 33% of the attendants of the ball turned into pumpkins, then "for each 100" attendants, 33 turned into pumpkins. Seeing a percent sign behind a number is the same thing as seeing a number over 100 $\left(x\% = \frac{x}{100}\right)$. For example, $100\% = \frac{100}{100} = 1$. Percents are simply an alternative (and common) means of expressing fractions whose denominators are 100. $25\% = \frac{25}{100}$ and $32\% = \frac{32}{100}$ and $150\% = \frac{150}{100}$. If Derrick buys 25% of his clothes at The Unlimited, Derrick buys $\frac{25}{100}$ or a fourth of his clothes at The Unlimited.

Conversions to Percents

To convert <u>fractions</u> to <u>percents</u>:

(1) multiply the fraction times 100
(2) divide the resulting numerator by the denominator
(3) add the % sign

$$\frac{2}{5} \times \frac{100}{1} = \frac{200}{5} \qquad 5\overline{)200}^{\,40\%}$$

To convert <u>decimals</u> to <u>percents</u>:

(1) multiply the decimal times 100 by moving the decimal over two spots to the right
(2) add the % sign

.33 = 33%

Conversions from Percents

To convert <u>percents</u> to <u>fractions</u>:

(1) drop the % sign
(2) put the remaining number over 100

$$62\% = \frac{62}{100}$$

To convert <u>percents</u> to <u>decimals</u>:

(1) drop the % sign
(2) divide the remaining number by 100 by moving the decimal point over two spots to the left

32% = .32

A consideration: If you lose your bearings when working with percents, decimals and/or fractions, think back on the easy-to-understand relationships, such as $100\% = 1.0 = \frac{100}{100}$, $50\% = .5 = \frac{50}{100}$, and $25\% = \frac{25}{100} = .25$. These relationships will remind you of the nature of the connections between percents, decimals and fractions.

PRACTICE SET 12

Convert the following values to percentages:

1. 0.51

2. 5.1

3. 0.051

4. 0.0051

5. $\dfrac{1}{3}$

6. $\dfrac{4}{3}$

7. $\dfrac{21}{25}$

8. $\dfrac{1}{8}$

9. $\dfrac{1}{4}$

Convert the following percentages to decimal form:

10. 92%

11. 9.2%

12. 920%

13. 4%

14. 0.1%

Convert the following percentages to reduced fractions:

15. 65%

16. 120%

17. 0.08%

18. 10%

19. 75%

ANSWERS AND EXPLANATIONS—PRACTICE SET 12

1. 51%   .51 = 51%

2. 510%   5.10 = 510%

3. 5.1%   0.051 = 5.1%

4. 0.51%   0.0051 = .51%

5. ≈ 33.3%

$$\frac{1}{3} \times 100 = \frac{100}{3}$$

```
       33.3...
    3)100.0
       9
       10
        9
       10
        9
        1
```

6. ≈ 133.3%

$$\frac{4}{3} \times 100 = \frac{400}{3}$$

```
       133.3...
    3)400.0
       3
       10
        9
       10
        9
       10
        9
        1
```

7. 84%

$$\frac{21}{25} \times 100 = \frac{2100}{25}$$

```
        84
    25)2100
       200
       100
       100
         0
```

8. 12.5%

$$\frac{1}{8} \times 100 = \frac{100}{8}$$

$$\begin{array}{r} 12.5 \\ 8\overline{\smash{)}100.0} \\ \underline{8} \\ 20 \\ \underline{16} \\ 40 \\ \underline{40} \\ 0 \end{array}$$

9. 25%

$$\frac{1}{4} \times 100 = \frac{100}{4}$$

$$\begin{array}{r} 25 \\ 4\overline{\smash{)}100} \\ \underline{8} \\ 20 \\ \underline{20} \\ 0 \end{array}$$

10. 0.92   92% = .92

11. 0.092   9.2% = .092

12. 9.2   920% = 9.2

13. 0.04   4% = .04

14 0.001   0.1% = .001

15. $\frac{13}{20}$ $65\% = .65 = \frac{65}{100} = \frac{13}{20}$

16. $\frac{6}{5}$ $120\% = \frac{120}{100} = \frac{6}{5}$

17. $\frac{1}{1,250}$ $0.08\% = \frac{0.08}{100} = \frac{8}{10000} = \frac{1}{1250}$

18. $\frac{1}{10}$ $10\% = \frac{10}{100} = \frac{1}{10}$

19. $\frac{3}{4}$ $75\% = \frac{75}{100} = \frac{3}{4}$

Part/Percent/Whole Problems

Many percent problems can be solved with the following formula:

part = percent × whole

Given any two of the above, you can find the third. Once you determine what's given and what's not, you can manipulate the above formula to suit your needs:

part = percent × whole

$$percent = \frac{part}{whole}$$

$$whole = \frac{part}{percent}$$

Sample Question 13: What is 35% of 65?

Process (words)	Process (numbers)
(1) determine what is being asked for	(1) part
(2) given what's being asked for, determine formula	(2) part = percent × whole
(3) set up the equation	(3) part = 35% × 65
(4) convert percent to decimal	(4) part = .35 × 65
(5) perform the operations	(5) part = .35 × 65 part = 22.75

Sample Question 14: What percent of 320 is 128?

Process (words)	Process (numbers)
(1) determine what is being asked for	(1) percent
(2) given what's being asked for determine formula	(2) $percent = \frac{part}{whole}$
(3) set up the equation	(3) $percent = \frac{128}{320}$
(4) perform the operations	(4) $percent = \frac{128}{320}$

percent = .4

(5) convert decimal to percent   (4) percent = .4
                                           percent = 40%

Sample Question 15: 400 is 75% of what number?

Process (words)   Process (numbers)

(1) determine what is being asked for   (1) whole

(2) given what's being asked for   (2) $whole = \dfrac{part}{percent}$
    determine formula

(3) set up the equation   (3) $whole = \dfrac{400}{75\%}$

(4) convert percent to decimal   (4) $whole = \dfrac{400}{.75}$

(5) convert decimal denominator to   (5) $whole = \dfrac{400}{.75} \times \dfrac{100}{100}$
    whole number $whole = \dfrac{40,000}{75}$

(6) perform the operations   (6) $whole = \dfrac{40,000}{75}$
                                            $whole = 533.333...$

Now let's try some *real* word problems:

Sample Question 16: If 93.75% of The Dream Team is made up of professional players, and there are 16 players on The Dream Team, how many of them are professional players?

Process (words)	Process (numbers)
(1) determine what is being asked for	(1) professional part of The Dream Team
(2) given what's being asked for determine formula	(2) part = percent × whole
(3) set up the equation	(3) part = 93.75% × 16
(4) convert percent to decimal	(4) part = .9375 × 16
(5) perform the operations	(5) part = .9375 × 16 part = 15

Sample Question 17: If 920 of the 1500 tickets to the Dizrithmia concert have been sold, approximately what percentage of the tickets have been sold?

Process (words)	Process (numbers)
(1) determine what is being asked for	(1) approximate percent of tickets sold
(2) given what's being asked for determine formula	(2) $percent = \dfrac{part}{whole}$
(3) set up the equation	(3) $percent = \dfrac{920}{1,500}$
(4) perform the operations	(4) $percent = \dfrac{920}{1,500}$ percent = .61333...
(5) convert decimal to percent and round	(5) percent = .61333 percent ≈ 61%

Sample Question 18:   If I spent 25% of my allowance at the ball game today, and I bought only a baseball cap for $5.25, a coke for $1.00 and a popcorn for $1.50, how much was my allowance?

Process (words)	Process (numbers)
(1) determine what is being asked for	(1) whole allowance
(2) given what's being asked for determine formula	(2) $whole = \dfrac{part}{percent}$
(3) set up the equation	(3) $whole = \dfrac{7.75}{25\%}$
(4) convert percent to decimal	(4) $whole = \dfrac{7.75}{.25}$
(5) convert decimal denominator to whole number	(5) $whole = \dfrac{7.75}{.25} \times \dfrac{100}{100}$ $whole = \dfrac{775}{25}$
(6) perform the operations	(6) $whole = \dfrac{775}{25} = \$31$

PRACTICE SET 13

1. What is 45% of 20?

2. What is 110% of 70?

3. What percent of 175 is 70?

4. What percent of 20 is 15?

5. 180 is 12% of what?

6. 115 is 250% of what?

7. What percent of 125 is 120?

8. What is 20% of 80?

9. 138 is 23% of what?

10. If there are 5 vowels in an alphabet of 26 letters, what percentage of the alphabet is composed of vowels?

11. A company claims that 80% of shoppers prefer Product A over Product B. If this claim was based on a survey of 4,480 shoppers, how many shoppers in the survey preferred Product A?

12. A candidate received 3,230 votes in an election. If this turned out to be 34% of all votes cast, then a total of how many people voted in the election?

13. A particular neighborhood has 84 residents who could all speak English and/or Spanish. 78 of the residents could speak English, 55 could speak Spanish, and 49 could speak both English and Spanish. What percent of English speakers could also speak Spanish?

14. A student answered 76% of the questions on an exam correctly. He answered 19 questions correctly. What was the total number of questions on the exam?

15. A contract was sold for $27,360. Sharon received a 12% commission for selling the contract. How much did she receive?

72

ANSWERS AND EXPLANATIONS—PRACTICE SET 13

1. 9   part   = percent × whole

$$= (.45)(20)$$
$$= 9$$

2. 77   part   = percent × whole

$$= (1.10)(70)$$
$$= 77$$

3. 40%   percent $= \dfrac{\text{part}}{\text{whole}}$

$$= \frac{70}{175} = .40$$
$$= 40\%$$

4. 75%   percent $= \dfrac{\text{part}}{\text{whole}}$

$$= \frac{15}{20} = .75$$
$$= 75\%$$

5. 1,500   whole $= \dfrac{\text{part}}{\text{percent}}$

$$= \frac{180}{.12}$$
$$= 1,500$$

6. 46   whole $= \dfrac{\text{part}}{\text{percent}}$

$$= \frac{115}{2.50}$$
$$= 46$$

7. 96%   percent $= \dfrac{\text{part}}{\text{whole}}$

$$= \frac{120}{125} = .96$$
$$= 96\%$$

8. 16   part $= \text{percent} \times \text{whole}$

$= (.20)\,(80)$

$= 16$

9. 600   whole $= \dfrac{\text{part}}{\text{percent}}$

$= \dfrac{138}{.23}$

$= 600$

10. $\approx 19.2\%$. The question asks for the percent of the alphabet that is composed of vowels. The "whole" is the alphabet and the "part" is the collective vowels:

$$\text{percent} = \dfrac{\text{part}}{\text{whole}}$$

$$= \dfrac{5}{26}$$

$$\approx .192$$

$$\approx 19.2\%$$

11. 3,584. The question asks for the "part" of the shoppers preferring Product A. The "whole" is all the shoppers surveyed and the "percentage" is given:

$$\text{part} = \text{percent} \times \text{whole}$$

$$= (.80)\,(4,480)$$

$$= 3,584$$

12. 9,500. The question asks for the "total" or "whole" number of people voting in the election. The "part" of votes the candidate received and the percentage are given:

$$\text{whole} = \dfrac{\text{part}}{\text{percent}}$$

$$= \dfrac{3,230}{.34}$$

$$= 9,500$$

13. ≈ 62.8. The question asks for the percentage of English speakers who can also speak Spanish. The "whole" is the number of English speakers, and the "part" is the number of Spanish and English speakers (bilinguals):

$$\text{percent} = \frac{\text{part}}{\text{whole}}$$

$$= \frac{49}{78} \approx .628$$

$$\approx 62.8\%$$

14. 25. The question asks for the "total" of "whole" number of questions on the exam. The "percent" and "part" are given:

$$\text{whole} = \frac{\text{part}}{\text{percent}}$$

$$= \frac{19}{.76}$$

$$= 25$$

15. 3,283.20. The question asks for the "part" Sharon received:

$$\text{part} = \text{percent} \times \text{whole}$$

$$= (.12)(27,360)$$

$$= 3283.20$$

Percent Change Problems

Sometimes, you'll be asked to determine percent increase or percent decrease, say of ticket sales, populations or prices. The basic formula for solving percent change problems is:

$$\% \text{ change} = \frac{\text{amount of change}}{\text{original amount}} \times \frac{100}{1}$$

There's a version of this for increase, and one for decrease:

$$\% \text{ increase} = \frac{\text{new amount} - \text{original amount}}{\text{original amount}} \times \frac{100}{1}$$

$$\% \text{ decrease} = \frac{\text{original amount} - \text{new amount}}{\text{original amount}} \times \frac{100}{1}$$

Sample Question 19: 306 tickets were sold at last week's Sockadillos game. 420 tickets were sold at last night's game. What is the percent increase?

Process (words)	Process (numbers)
(1) determine what is being asked for	(1) % increase
(2) given what's being asked for determine formula	(2) $\% \text{ increase} = \dfrac{\text{increase \#}}{\text{original \#}} \times 100$ $\dfrac{\text{new amount} - \text{original amount}}{\text{original amount}} \times \dfrac{100}{1}$ $\dfrac{420 - 306}{306} \times \dfrac{100}{1}$
(3) set up the equation	(3) $\% \text{ increase} = \dfrac{114}{306} \times 100$
(4) perform operations	(4) $\% \text{ increase} = \dfrac{11,400}{306}$ $\% \text{ increase} \approx 37\%$

Sample Question 20: If a pair of overalls originally costs $63.00, but has been marked down to $56.70, what percent is the markdown?

Process (words)	Process (numbers)
(1) determine what is being asked for	(1) % decrease
(2) given what's being asked for determine formula	(2) $\% \text{ decrease} = \dfrac{\text{decrease \#}}{\text{original \#}} \times 100$ $\dfrac{\text{original amount} - \text{new amount}}{\text{original amount}} \times \dfrac{100}{1}$ $\dfrac{63 - 56.7}{63} \times \dfrac{100}{1}$
(3) set up the equation	(3) $\% \text{ decrease} = \dfrac{6.3}{63} \times 100$
(4) perform operations	(4) $\% \text{ decrease} = \dfrac{630}{63}$ $\% \text{ decrease} = 10\%$

Other Percent Problems

1. New Price: Suppose you are told that a $1000 bike has been marked down 75%, and you want to find the new price. You don't need a formula to solve this—just use common sense. The new price will be 25% (it's been marked *down* 75% of the original price). $.25 \times 1000 = 250$, so the sale price is $250. If the numbers aren't so cut and dry, use the following formulas to figure adjusted price:

$$\text{Decrease or Increase} = \text{Original Price}\left(\frac{\%\ \text{Markdown}}{\text{Markup}}\right)$$

New Price = Original Price − Decrease

New Price = Original Price + Increase

2. Subsequent Adjustments: Suppose you are told a $1000 bike was initially marked down 75% and then a week later marked down an additional 7%, and you wanted to find the new price. Since the second markdown was *not* on $1000, but rather on $250, you cannot simply figure out what an 82% discount on $1000 would be. Since 7% of 250 is 17.50, the final sale price of the bike is $250 − $17.50 or $232.50. (If you totaled the markdown percentages before figuring, you ended up with a final, and wrong, price of $180.)

3. Original Price: You could be asked to figure out the original price of a bike that, at a 75% discount, costs $250. Again, use common sense. You know what 25% of the bike costs, so multiply that amount times 4, and you'll have 100% of the original cost. $250 × 4 = $1000. Here are the formulas for the more challenging numbers:

$$\text{Original Price} = \frac{\text{New Price}}{100\% - \%\text{Markdown}}$$

$$\text{Original Price} = \frac{\text{New Price}}{100\% + \%\text{Markup}}$$

Fraction/Decimal/Percent chart:

$\frac{1}{2} = .5 = 50\%$

$\frac{1}{3} = .33... = 33\frac{1}{3}\%$

$\frac{2}{3} = .66... = 66\frac{2}{3}\%$

$\frac{1}{4} = .25 = 25\%$

$\frac{3}{4} = .75 = 75\%$

$\frac{1}{5} = .2 = 20\%$

$$\frac{2}{5} = .4 = 40\%$$

$$\frac{3}{5} = .6 = 60\%$$

$$\frac{4}{5} = .8 = 80\%$$

4. Simple Interest: If $3,500 is deposited into an account at 6% simple annual interest, how much interest would the account earn after 4 months? To calculate simple interest after one year multiply the interest and the principle:

$$.06 \times 3,500 = \$210$$

But 4 months, is only $\frac{1}{3}$ of a year:

$$\frac{1}{3} \times 210 = \$70$$

5. Compound Interest: If interest is compounded, then the computation must include both the principle and any interest already earned in previous periods. Remember to divide the interest rate by the number of periods in a year. If the interest is compounded semi-annually divide it by 2. If it is compounded quarterly, divide it by 4.

Suppose you are asked to find the interest earned by $500 at 12% interest, compounded quarterly after 6 months. The interest is compounded quarterly so every 3 months $\left(\frac{3}{12} = \frac{1}{4}\right)$ the sum earns $\left(\frac{1}{4}\right)(12\%) = 3\%$ interest. After the first three months the interest earned is $(.03)(500) = \$15$. The interest earned from the first 3 months must be included when calculating the interest earned from the second three months:

$$(.03)(500 + 15) = (.03)(515) = \$15.45$$

So the total interest earned after 6 months is $15 + 15.45 = \$30.45$.

PRACTICE SET 14

1. Last year the Robotic Paper clip Corporation spent $3,000,000 on research. This year the research budget was expanded to $3,960,000. What percentage increase was made in research spending?

2. In a coastal area shortly before a hurricane, it was estimated that there were 20 squirrels per acre. Immediately after the hurricane it was estimated that there were only 8 squirrels per acre. What was the percent decrease in the estimated squirrel population density of that area?

3. When negotiating the purchase of a new car, the car dealer tells you she is willing to knock 16% off the list price of $12,000. What is the new price?

4. The same car dealer offers to knock an additional 10% off the offer she made in question 3 above. What is the new offer?

5. A friend has 36 CDs in his apartment. He tells you he has more, but 25% of his CD collection has been loaned out. If this percentage is accurate, how many CDs does he have loaned out?

6. If $2,000 is invested at 12% interest, compounded semiannually, what is the balance after one year?

ANSWERS AND EXPLANATIONS—PRACTICE SET 14

1. **32%** The question asks for a percent increase, so we plug the new amount, 3,960,000 and the original amount, 3,000,000 into the formula:

$$\% \text{ increase} = \frac{3,960,000 - 3,000,000}{3,000,000} \times 100 = 32\%$$

2. **60%** The question asks for a percent decrease, so we plug the original density, 20, and the new density, 8, into the formula:

$$\% \text{ decrease} = \frac{20 - 8}{20} \times 100 = 60\%$$

3. **$10,080** The direct way to solve this problem is to calculate how much 16% of the original price is and deduct that amount:

$$\text{part} = \text{percent} \times \text{whole}$$
$$= .16 \times 12,000)$$
$$= 1,920$$

$$12,000 - 1,920 = 10,080$$

4. **$9,072** Here it is important to remember to take 10% off the $10,080 (the new offer) and not to add the 10% to the 16% (which would result in an error).

5. First, determine the "whole" or total number of CDs. You know that 75% of the whole CD collection is represented by 36 CDs because 25% are loaned out and 100% − 25% = 75%.

$$\text{whole} = \frac{\text{part}}{\text{percent}}$$

$$\text{whole} = \frac{36}{.75}$$

$$\text{whole} = 48$$

Now determine what 25% of 48 is:

$$\text{part} = (.25)\,48$$
$$\text{part} = 12$$

6. **$2,247.20** Interest compounded semiannually is compounded twice a year. Every 6 months the investment earns $\left(\frac{1}{2}\right)(12\%) = 6\%$. After the first 6 months the interest earned is $(.06)(2,000) = \$120$. The new balance is $2,000 + 120 = \$2,120$. The interest earned for the second 6 months is $(.06)(2,120) = \$127.20$. Thus the final balance is $2,120 + 127.20 = \$2,247.20$.

Ratios

Ratio Types

A *ratio* is an expression of *comparison* through division. Fractions are ratios, and ratios can and should be written as, and treated as, fractions. Ratios are usually reduced to their lowest form. If you encounter an unreduced ratio, reduce it *before* you work with it, just as you would a fraction. The ratio 2:3 can be written $\frac{2}{3}$ and treated exactly like the fraction $\frac{2}{3}$. Here are two kinds of comparisons that are related through ratios:

1. *Part to Part Ratios*. These ratios express a relationship between two parts. Suppose that, in a certain room, there are 2 fundamentalists to every 3 atheists. This is a part to part ratio, and it would be expressed 2:3 or $\frac{2}{3}$.

2. *Part to Whole Ratios*. These ratios express a relationship between a part and its whole, just as a fraction expresses a relationship between a part (the numerator) and its whole (the denominator). For instance, if there are exactly five people in the room discussed above the ratio of fundamentalists (part) to people in the room (whole) would be 2:5, and the ratio of atheists (part) to people in the room (whole) would be 3:5. (This is the same as saying $\frac{2}{5}$ of the people in the room are fundamentalists, and $\frac{3}{5}$ are atheists.)

Figuring the Real Numbers of Parts

Suppose you are told that a certain 15 member softball team is comprised of boys and girls, and that the ratio of boys to girls on the team is 1:4. That ratio is comprised of parts that are *mutually exclusive*; that is, there is *no overlap* between the parts. No boys are girls and no girls are boys. Since you're told that there are only boys and girls on the team, you can deduce also that the parts in the ratio account for the *entire* team. There are no parts to the whole (the team) except the girl parts and the boy parts. Such information can be used to determine the real numbers behind the parts—the exact number of boys and the exact number of girls on the team. If you encounter ratios that are (1) mutually exclusive (part to part with no overlap) and (2) comprising of the entire whole (the whole = only the sum of the parts related), then you can figure out the real numbers behind the parts.

To distribute a whole across a ratio:

(1) count the total parts (1 part boy + 4 parts girl = 5 total parts)
(2) divide the number given (the whole) by the number of total parts (15 ÷ 5 = 3)
(3) take that quotient and multiply it by each side of the ratio (3 × 1 = 3 boys and 3 × 4 = 12 girls)

Sample Question 21: If there are 25 people in a room in which the ratio of fundamentalists to atheists is 2:3, and if we know that there are no people other than fundamentalists and atheists in the room, exactly how many fundamentalists, and how many atheists are there in the room?

Process (words)	Process (numbers)
(1) count the total parts	(1) $2 + 3 = 5$
(2) divide the number given by the number of total parts	(2) $25 \div 5 = 5$
(3) multiply the quotient by each side of the ratio	(3) $5 \times 2 = 10$ (there are 10 fundamentalists) $5 \times 3 = 15$ (there are 15 atheists)

A consideration: It's reasonable to assume that there's no overlap between fundamentalists and atheists (the parts in the ratio are mutually exclusive), and we're given that there are only fundamentalists and atheists in the room (the parts in the ratio make up the whole), so we <u>can</u> figure out the real numbers of the parts. If instead we were told that there are also agnostics in the room, we *couldn't* figure out the real numbers of the parts, because we don't know anything about *how many* agnostics there are in the room (the parts in the ratio don't make up the whole).

Three Part Ratios

Sometimes you will encounter three part ratios. Treat these just as you would two part ratios:

Sample Question 22: If there are 30 people in a room in which the ratio of fundamentalists to atheists to agnostics is 2:3:5, and if we know that there are no people other than fundamentalists, atheists and agnostics in the room, exactly how many of each are there in the room?

Process (words)	Process (numbers)
(1) count the total parts	(1) $2 + 3 + 5 = 10$
(2) divide the number given by the number of total parts	(2) $30 \div 10 = 3$
(3) multiply the quotient by all parts of the ratio	(3) $3 \times 2 = 6$ (there are 6 fundamentalists) $3 \times 3 = 9$ (there are 9 atheists) $3 \times 5 = 15$ (there are 15 agnostics)

A consideration: If you're given two separate part to part ratios, in which one of the parts is common, you can treat the two as one three part ratio, provided that the like part is the same number in both ratios. (A fundamentalist to atheist ratio of 2:3 plus an atheist to agnostic ratio of 3:5 = a fundamentalist to atheist to agnostic ratio of 2:3:5.) If the common part is not the same, make it the same by treating the part as a common denominator. (A fundamentalist to atheist ratio of 1:2 plus an atheist to agnostic ratio of 4:5 = a fundamentalist to atheist to agnostic ratio of 2:4:5.)

Ratios that are Equal

Ratios that are equal form a *proportion*. $\frac{4}{5} = \frac{8}{10}$ is a proportion. 4, 5, 8, and 10 are the *terms* of the proportion. Frequently, you will encounter questions which test your ability to find the missing term of a proportion. To do this, set the ratios up as fractions and then cross multiply and solve for the missing term:

$$\frac{4}{5} = \frac{x}{10}$$

$40 = 5x$ (cross multiply)

$$\frac{40}{5} = x$$

$$x = 8$$

$$\frac{4}{5} = \frac{8}{10}$$

Direct Proportions

The quantities in a *direct* proportion, such as the example above, vary directly: they change in the *same* direction. As one gets larger, the other gets larger and as one gets smaller, the other gets smaller. For example the *more* pieces of 5 cent gum you buy, the *more* money you spend. Ratios involving cost per quantity usually form a direct proportion:

If 1 piece of gum costs 5 cents, how much would 6 pieces of gum cost:

$$\frac{1 \text{ piece}}{6 \text{ pieces}} = \frac{5 \text{ cents}}{x \text{ cents}}$$

$$1x = 30$$

$$x = 30$$

$$\frac{1 \text{ piece}}{6 \text{ pieces}} = \frac{5 \text{ cents}}{30 \text{ cents}}$$

6 pieces would cost 30 cents

A consideration: This proportion could be set up with the unlike terms grouped in a single ratio: $\frac{1 \text{ piece}}{5 \text{ cents}} = \frac{6 \text{ pieces}}{x \text{ cents}}$. Proportions are flexible in this way; the two arrangements are mathematically the same.

Inverse Proportions

The terms in an *inverse* proportion vary indirectly: they change in *opposite* directions. As one gets larger, the other gets smaller. For example, if a job takes 6 labor-hours, the *more* workers there are on it, the *less* amount of time it takes. Ratios involving number of workers per job completion time usually form an inverse proportion, which is set up like a direct proportion except that one of the ratios is inverted:

How long would it take for 6 workers to do a job that can be completed by 1 worker in 6 hours?

$$\frac{1 \text{ worker}}{6 \text{ workers}} = \frac{x \text{ hours}}{6 \text{ hours}} \quad \text{(the second ratio is inverted)}$$

$$6 = 6x$$

$$x = 1$$

$$\frac{1 \text{ worker}}{6 \text{ workers}} = \frac{1 \text{ hour}}{6 \text{ hours}}$$

6 workers could complete the job in 1 hour

Common sense will help you figure out when proportions are direct or inverse. Consider whether or not the relationships involved in these scenarios form a direct or an inverse proportion:

1. An increase in quantity results in an increase in weight. D or I?

2. A faster speed results in less travel time for a given trip. D or I?

3. A smaller ball takes more revolutions to travel a given distance. D or I?

4. A car payment is lower when extended over a longer period. D or I?

Here are the answers with examples:

1. An *increase* in quantity results in an *increase* in weight. The quantities vary in the *same* direction so the proportion would be direct:

   If a gallon of water weighs 8 lbs., how much does 15 gallons of water weigh?

   $$\frac{1 \text{ gallon}}{15 \text{ gallons}} = \frac{8 \text{ lbs.}}{x \text{ lbs.}}$$

   $$x = 120$$

   $$\frac{1 \text{ gallon}}{15 \text{ gallons}} = \frac{8 \text{ lbs.}}{120 \text{ lbs.}}$$

   15 gallons of water weigh 120 lbs.

2. A *faster* speed results in *less* travel time. The quantities vary in *opposite* directions so the proportion would be inverse:

A train traveling 60 mph takes 3 hours to make a certain trip. How long would the trip take if the train were traveling at 180 mph?

$$\frac{60 \text{ mph}}{180 \text{ mph}} = \frac{x \text{ hours}}{3 \text{ hours}} \quad \text{(the second ratio is inverted)}$$

$$180 = 180x$$

$$x = 1$$

$$\frac{60 \text{ mph}}{180 \text{ mph}} = \frac{1 \text{ hour}}{3 \text{ hours}}$$

the trip would take 1 hour

3. A *smaller* ball would take *more* revolutions to travel a given distance. The quantities vary in *opposite* directions so the proportion would be inverse:

A ball with a circumference of 12 inches takes 10 revolutions to travel from point A to point B. How many revolutions would it take a ball with a circumference of 3 inches to travel the same amount?

$$\frac{12 \text{ inches}}{3 \text{ inches}} = \frac{x \text{ revolutions}}{10 \text{ revolutions}} \quad \text{(the second ratio is inverted)}$$

$$120 = 3x$$

$$x = 40$$

$$\frac{12 \text{ inches}}{3 \text{ inches}} = \frac{40 \text{ revolutions}}{10 \text{ revolutions}}$$

the smaller ball would take 40 revolutions

4. A car payment is *lower* when extended over a *longer* period. The quantities vary in *opposite* directions so the proportion would be inverse:

A car payment is $350 a month for a 26 month period. How much would it be for a 40 month period?

$$\frac{26 \text{ months}}{40 \text{ months}} = \frac{x \text{ dollars}}{350 \text{ dollars}}$$

$$9,100 = 40x$$

$$x = \frac{9,100}{40}$$

$$x = 227.50$$

$$\frac{26 \text{ months}}{40 \text{ months}} = \frac{227.50 \text{ dollars}}{350 \text{ dollars}}$$

the payment over a 40 month period would be $227.50

PRACTICE SET 15

1. Last Friday a doctor saw 33 patients. The ratio of male to female patients was 6 to 5. How many patients of each sex were there?

2. On a cruise ship the ratio of passengers to crew members was 15:1. The number of passengers and crew members on board totaled 800. How many passengers were there? How many crew members?

3. In the middle of a checkers game, the ratio of red checkers to black checkers was 3:2. There were 15 checkers on the board at that time. What fraction of the checkers were red? What fraction of the checkers were black? How many of each color were there?

4. All of the cars parked at a parking lot were made in Europe, Asia, or the United States. The ratio of European cars to American cars was 1:2. The ratio of American cars to Asian cars was 4:3. There were 36 cars in the parking lot. How many cars of each origin were there?

5. If $9 dollars bought 4 cheeseburgers, how many could have been bought with $13.50?

6. If 6 pumps can empty a tank in 3 hours, how long would it take 1 pump to empty the tank?

7. Last Thursday at a coffee shop the ratio of coffees served to teas served was 7:3. Last Thursday the coffee shop served 54 teas. How many coffees were served that day?

ANSWERS AND EXPLANATIONS—PRACTICE SET 15

1. 18 male, 15 female. Counting the total parts gives: $6 + 5 = 11$. Dividing the number of patients by the total parts gives: $33 \div 11 = 3$. So, 3×6 gives the number of males, and 3×5 gives the number of females.

2. 750 passengers, 50 crew members. Using the same strategy as the preceding problem we get the total parts: $15 + 1 = 16$, and divide into the number on board: $800 \div 16 = 50$. So, $50 \times 15 = 750$ given the number of passengers, and $50 \times 1 = 50$ gives the number of crew.

3. $\frac{3}{5}$ were red, $\frac{2}{5}$ were black, 9 red, 6 black. Counting the total parts gives: $3 + 2 = 5$. The red "part" is 3, so $\frac{3}{5}$ of the checkers are red. The black "part" is 2, so $\frac{2}{5}$ of the checkers are black. Taking the total parts and dividing it into the total number of checkers gives: $15 \div 5 = 3$. So $3 \times 3 = 9$ red checkers, and $3 \times 2 = 6$ black checkers.

4. 8 European, 16 American, 12 Asian. The common part of the two ratios given is the American cars category. Treating the American cars part as a common denominator, the first ratio is converted from 1:2 to 2:4. A three part ratio can now be built. The European to American to Asian ratio is 2:4:3. The total parts are $2 + 4 + 3 = 9$. Dividing the total number of cars gives $36 \div 9 = 4$. So, $4 \times 2 = 8$ European, $4 \times 4 = 16$ American, and $4 \times 3 = 12$ Asian cars.

5. 6 burgers. This is a direct proportion problem:

    $$\frac{9 \text{ dollars}}{13.50 \text{ dollars}} = \frac{4 \text{ burgers}}{x \text{ burgers}}$$

    cross multiplying yields:

    $$9x = (4)(13.50)$$
    $$x = \frac{4(13.50)}{9}$$
    $$x = \frac{54}{9}$$
    $$x = 6$$

6. 18 hours. This is an inverse proportion problem because the more pumps that are working, the less time it takes to pump the tank.

    $$\frac{6 \text{ pumps}}{1 \text{ pump}} = \frac{x}{3 \text{ hours}}$$

    Notice that the right side fraction is inverted. Cross multiplying yields $18 = x$.

7. 126. This can be viewed as a direct proportion problem. The two tea "parts" are 3 (from the ratio) and 54. The two coffee "parts" are 7 (from the ratio) and x.

    $$\frac{3 \text{ teas}}{54 \text{ teas}} = \frac{7 \text{ coffees}}{x}$$

cross multiplying yields:

$$3x = 7(54)$$

$$x = \frac{7(54)}{3}$$

$$x = \frac{378}{3}$$

$$x = 126$$

Averages

Simple Average

The *average* or *arithmetic mean* of a group of numbers is the sum of the group divided by the number of terms in the group. This relationship can be expressed three different ways:

$$\text{average} = \frac{\text{sum}}{\text{number}}$$

Suppose Johnny took 5 tests over the course of the semester. If Johnny made a 75 on tests 1, 2 and 3, an 80 on test 4 and a 100 on test 5, what is his average test grade?

$$\text{average} = \frac{(75 + 75 + 75 + 80 + 100)}{5}$$

$$\text{average} = \frac{405}{5}$$

$$\text{average} = 81$$

$$\text{sum} = \text{average} \times \text{number}$$

If Daniel's three children Jess, Willie and Sara spent an average of $130 each on clothes for the new school year, how much did they spend collectively?

sum = $130 × 3
sum = $390

$$\text{number} = \frac{\text{sum}}{\text{average}}$$

If Seymour made $600 scalping tickets outside the arena, and he averaged $15 per ticket, how many tickets did he sell?

$$\text{number} = \frac{\$600}{\$15}$$

number = 40

Sample Question 23: What is the arithmetic mean of the consecutive integers 1 through 10?

<u>Process (words)</u>   <u>Process (numbers)</u>

(1) add the numbers (to find the sum)

(1) sum = $1 + 2 + 3 + 4 + 5 + 6 + 7 + 8 + 9 + 10$
    sum = 55

(2) count the numbers (to find the number)

(2) number = 10

(3) determine the average

(3) average = $\dfrac{\text{sum}}{\text{number}}$

   average = $\dfrac{55}{10}$

   average = 5.5

A consideration: All 12 numbers in the group that you are averaging *carry equal weight.* Suppose you ordered CD's, 4 of which cost $10, 4 of which cost $11 and 4 of which cost $15. How much was your average cost per CD? $40 + $44 + $60 = $144. $\frac{\$144}{12} = \$12$.

Your average cost per CD was $12. Suppose then you ordered 1 more CD, which cost $10, what is your new average cost per CD? It wouldn't be 11 unless you bought 12 $10 CD's instead of 1 because *each number carries equal weight.* Simply figure out the *new* sum ($144 + $10 = $154), and divide it by the *new* number of terms $\left(\frac{\$154}{13} \approx \$11.85\right)$.

Missing Information

Some average problems ask you to determine a missing term in a group. You can solve for a missing term with subtraction or with a plus-minus chart:

1. **Subtraction**

If Haket averaged 3 goals per game over the course of a 5 game soccer tournament, and he scored 4 goals in the first and third games, 0 in second and 2 in the last, how many did he score in the fourth?

Haket must have scored $3 \times 5 = 15$ goals so 15 is the sum. We know he scored $4 + 4 + 0 + 2 = 10$ goals in 4 of the games, so he must have scored $15 - 10 = 5$ goals in the remaining game.

2. Plus-Minus Chart Method

Suppose Haket played in another tournament, this time a 6 game tournament, and that he averaged 2 goals per game. If he scored 1 goal in the first, 1 goal in the second, 3 goals in the third, 0 goals in the fourth and 4 goals in the fifth, how many did he score in the sixth?

game	# scored	compared to 2	left at
game 1	1 goal	-1	-1
game 2	1 goal	-1	-2
game 3	3 goals	+1	-1
game 4	0 goals	-2	-3
game 5	4 goals	+2	-1
game 6	3 goals	+1	0

Haket must have scored 3 goals in the final game, to make up for being 1 under the average after the 5th game.

Combined Averages

Finding a *combined* average of a set of averages is much like finding a simple average except that to find the sum you must <u>weight</u> each average by multiplying it by the number of terms it represents.

Sample Question 24:   If Haket's goal per game average was 3 in the spring, 1 in the summer and 2 in the fall, and he played 16 games in the spring, 9 in the summer and 25 in the fall, what was his goal per game average for the year?

Process (words)	Process (numbers)
(1) weight each average to determine sum	(1) $16 \times 3 = 48$ goals in the spring $9 \times 1 = 9$ goals in the summer $25 \times 2 = 50$ goals in the fall sum $= 48 + 9 + 50$ sum $= 107$
(2) determine the number	(2) number $= 16 + 9 + 25$ number $= 50$
(3) determine the average	(3) average $= \dfrac{107 \text{ goals}}{50 \text{ games}}$ average $= 2.14$ goals per game

92

Here is an example of a combined average problem, in which you are asked to determine a missing term:

Sample Question 25: If Tonita paid an average of 40 dollars apiece for 11 prints, and 8 of the prints averaged 16 dollars apiece, what did the remaining prints average?

Process (words)	Process (numbers)
(1) figure out the sum (average × number)	(1) sum = 40 × 11 sum = 440
(2) determine sub-sum #1	(2) sub-sum #1 = 8 × 16 sub-sum #1 = 128
(3) determine sub-sum #2	(3) sub-sum #2 = 440 − 128 sub-sum #2 = 312
(4) determine average #2	(4) average $= \dfrac{312}{3}$ average = \$104

Median

The median of a set of values is the value in a set below and above which there are an equal number of values. For a set in which there is an *odd* number of values, the median equals the exact *middle* value, and for a set in which there is an *even* number of values, the median equals the *average* of the two innermost values.

Here are a few examples:

1.   The median of 1, 2, 3, 4, and 5 is 3.
2.   The median of 10, 15, 16, 17, 32, 96, and 100 is 17.
3.   The median of 3, 8, 10, and 62 is 9.
4.   The median of 10, 32, 18, 56, 432, 8 and 6 is 18.

A consideration: Sometimes the median of a set = the mean of a set, as in #1.

Averaging Consecutive Integers

You might have noticed in Sample Question 23 that the average of the consecutive integers 1 through 10 ended up being the average of the two innermost integers (5 and 6). Here are three things to remember about averaging:

1.   The average of a group of consecutive or evenly spaced integers is always the exact middle number.
2.   If the number of integers in the group is *odd* the average is the middle integer.
3.   If the number of integers in the group is *even* the middle number is the average of the two innermost integers.

And a few examples:

The average of 6, 8, 10, 12, 14, 16 and 18 is 12.
The average of 567, 582 and 597 is 582.
The average of 4, 5, 6 and 7 is 5.5.
The average of 30, 100, 170, and 240 is 135.

Example: What is the average of the consecutive integers -1 through 9?

Process (words)	Process (numbers)
(1) count the integers	(1) -1, 0, 1, 2, 3, 4, 5, 6, 7, 8, 9 → 11 integers
(2) determine the middle integer	(2) "4" is the middle integer or average

(Sample Question 26 reminds you that zero *is* an integer.)

PRACTICE SET 16

1.   What is the average of 11, 23, 23, 14, 17, and 32?

2.   Amy took 4 trips averaging 1,400 miles a trip. How many total miles did she travel on these trips?

3.   Jake made $1,800 at a showing of his art. He made an average of $225 dollars per piece of art sold. How many pieces did he sell?

4.   The final grade in a course was determined by 3 exams. There were 2 midterm exams and a final exam that counted as 3 midterm exams. Amanda scored a 69 and a 76 on the midterms and a 95 on the final. What was her average at the end of the semester?

5.   Given a set of integers 28, 33, 45, and x, what must x be if the average of the set is 35?

6.   What is the average of each list of numbers?

   a.   2, 3, 4, 5, 6

   b.   2, 3, 4, 5

   c.   29, 31, 33, 35

   d.   -260, -258, -256, -254, -252, -250, -248

7.   What is the median of the set {20, 10, 8, 2}?

8.   What is the median of the set {66, 1000, 1}?

9.   What is the median of the set {5, 6, 7, 8}?

ANSWERS AND EXPLANATIONS—PRACTICE SET 16

1. 20.

$$\text{average} = \frac{\text{sum}}{\text{number}}$$

$$\frac{120}{6} = 20$$

2. 5,600.

$$\text{sum} = (\text{average}) \times (\text{number})$$
$$= 1,400 \times 4$$
$$= 5,600$$

3. 8.

$$\text{number} = \frac{\text{sum}}{\text{average}}$$
$$= \frac{1,800}{\$225}$$
$$= 8$$

4. 86. Since there are two midterms and a final worth three midterms, the problem can be viewed as a set of five midterms where the final score counted for three midterms.

first midterm	69
second midterm	76
final $3 \times 95 =$	285
sum	430

$$\text{average} = \frac{\text{sum}}{\text{number}}$$
$$= \frac{430}{5}$$
$$= 86$$

5. 34. For a set of 4 numbers to average 35, the number must sum to $4 \times 35 = 140$. Summing the known numbers gives: $28 + 33 + 45 = 106$. Subtracting this from what is needed, $140 - 106 = 34$, reveals that x must equal 34.

6. a. 4. An odd number of consecutive integers, so pick the middle term.

b. 3.5. An even number of consecutive integers, so pick the midpoint between the two middle terms (3 and 4).

c. 32. An even number of consecutive odd integers, so pick the midpoint between the two middle terms (31, 33).

d. -254. An odd number of consecutive even integers, so pick the middle term.

7. 9 Since there are 4 numbers, the median is the average of the middle numbers. The average of 10 and 8 is 9.

8. 66 Since there are 3 numbers, the median is the exact middle value. The exact middle value is 66.

9. 6.5 Since there are 4 numbers, the median is the average of the middle numbers. The average of 6 and 7 is 6.5.

PART 2: ALGEBRA

Exponents

Exponents Defined

An *exponent* is a little number up and to the right of a mathematical expression. The mathematical expression, which is oftentimes just a number, is called the *base*. An exponent tells you how many times you'll use the mathematical expression or base as a *factor*. 3^4, then, is $3 \times 3 \times 3 \times 3$ or 81. 3, here, has been raised to the 4th power. Numbers raised to the 2nd power are numbers *squared* and numbers raised to the 3rd power are numbers *cubed*.

Here are some other useful things to remember about exponents or *powers*:

1. A non-zero number raised to the 0 power equals 1:

    $$320^0 = 1 \text{ and } \left(\frac{1}{8}\right)^0 = 1$$

2. A number raised to the 1st power equals that number:

    $$62^1 = 62 \text{ and } 100^1 = 100$$

3. A fraction or decimal of a value between 0 and 1 raised to a positive power becomes smaller:

    $$\left(\frac{1}{4}\right)^2 = \frac{1}{16} \text{ and } (.25)^2 = .0625$$

4. 10 raised to a positive power equals 1 plus as many 0's as the exponent number:

    $$10^3 = 1,000 \text{ and } 10^8 = 100,000,000$$

5. A number raised to the power $\frac{1}{2}$ equals the square root of that number, and a number raised to the power $\frac{1}{3}$ equals the cubed root of that number:

    $$4^{\frac{1}{2}} = \sqrt{4} = \sqrt{2 \times 2} = 2$$
    $$27^{\frac{1}{3}} = \sqrt[3]{27} = \sqrt{3 \times 3 \times 3} = 3$$

    (square and cubed roots are covered extensively in the following section)

6. A negative number *in* parentheses raised to an even power equals a positive number:

    $$(-3)^2 = -3 \times -3 = 9$$

7. A negative number *in* parentheses raised to an odd power equals a negative number:

$(-3)^1 = -3$

8. A negative number *not* in parentheses raised to a power remains a negative:

$-3^2 = -(3)(3) = -9$ and $-2^2 = -(2)(2) = -4$

9. A number raised to a power which is in turn raised to a power equals that number raised to the product of the two powers:

$(5^2)^2 = 5^4$ and $(3^2)^6 = 3^{12}$

10. A number such as $\left(\frac{5}{3}\right)^2$ equals $\frac{5^2}{3^2}$ and a number such as $(3xy)^2 = 3^2x^2y^2$ (exponents on the outside of parentheses must be distributed to each term within the parentheses)

11. A number raised to a negative power equals the reciprocal of that number raised to the absolute value of the power indicated:

$4^{-2} = \left(\frac{1}{4}\right)^2 = \frac{1}{4} \times \frac{1}{4} = \frac{1}{16}$ and $\left(\frac{1}{2}\right)^{-3} = 2^3 = 2 \times 2 \times 2 = 8.$

Multiplication and Division with Exponents

Here are six things to remember about multiplication and division with exponents:

1. To multiply expressions in which the bases are the same, add the exponents:

$32^2 \times 32^6 = 32^8$

$$\left(\frac{1}{4}\right)^4 \times \left(\frac{1}{4}\right)^8 = \left(\frac{1}{4}\right)^{12}$$

2. To multiply expressions in which the exponents are the same, multiply the bases and then raise the product to the power indicated:

$5^5 \times 6^5 = (5 \times 6)^5 = 30^5 = 24,300,000$

3. To multiply expressions in which the bases and the exponents are different, figure out the value of each expression and then multiply:

$3^5 \times 6^2 = (3 \times 3 \times 3 \times 3 \times 3) \times (6 \times 6) = 243 \times 36 = 8,748$

4. To divide expressions in which the bases are the same, subtract the exponents:

$3^3 \div 3^2 = 3^{3-2} = 3^1$

$62^{16} \div 62^{14} = 62^{16-14} = 62^2 = 62 \times 62 = 3,844$

$$\frac{32^4}{32^1} = 32^{4-1} = 32^3 = 32 \times 32 \times 32 = 32,768$$

$$\frac{3^3}{3^4} = 3^{3-4} = 3^{-1} = \frac{1}{3}$$

5. To divide expressions in which the exponents are the same, divide the bases and then raise the quotient to the power indicated:

$$15^2 \div 5^2 = (15 \div 5)^2 = 3^2 = 9$$

6. To divide expressions in which the bases and the exponents are different, figure out the value of each expression and then divide:

$$16^2 \div 2^3 = (16 \times 16) \div (2 \times 2 \times 2) = 256 \div 8 = 32$$

Addition and Subtraction with Exponents

Here are two things to remember about addition and subtraction with exponents:

1. To add expressions figure out the value of each expression and then add:

$$5^2 + 3^2 = (5 \times 5) + (3 \times 3) = 25 + 9 = 34$$

$$3^3 + (-4)^2 = (3 \times 3 \times 3) + (-4 \times -4) = 27 + 16 = 43$$

2. To subtract expressions figure out the value of each expression and then subtract:

$$72^1 - 3^3 = (72) - (3 \times 3 \times 3) = 72 - 27 = 45$$

$$8^0 - 16^{\frac{1}{2}} = 1 - \sqrt{16} = 1 - 4 = -3$$

A consideration: Aside from factoring, which will be addressed in a subsequent section, there aren't any shortcuts to help you *add* or *subtract* numbers with exponents. Remember that the shortcuts apply to multiplication and division, and within those operations to numbers with like bases and/or like exponents only.

Comparisons of Numbers with Exponents

You need to be able to recognize the size of exponential numbers relative to one another. It's important to realize things like this:

1. 150^0 is less than 2^1

2. 32^2 is greater than 32×2

3. 3^5 is greater than 10^2

4. $\left(\frac{1}{5}\right)^{25}$ is less than 2^2

5. $(-555)^7$ is less than $(-555)^2$

6. $(-2)^3$ is greater than -2^8

7. $\left(\frac{1}{2}\right)^{50}$ is less than $\left(\frac{1}{2}\right)^{20}$

8. $(-15)^1$ is greater than $(-16)^1$

9. -3^3 is less than $(-3)^2$

10. $(-10)^2$ is greater than -10^2

Summary of the Rules of Exponents

(1) $x^y \times x^z = x^{y+z}$

(2) $x^y \div x^z = x^{y-z}$

(3) $x^y \times z^y = (x \times z)^y$

(4) $x^y \div z^y = (x \div z)^y$

(5) $(xy)^z = x^z y^z$

(6) $(x^y)^z = x^{yz}$

It would be a good idea to be familiar with the following squares of numbers 1 through 15 and cubes of numbers 1 through 5:

1^2	= 1	12^2	= 144	1^3	= 1
2^2	= 4	13^2	= 169	2^3	= 8
3^2	= 9	14^2	= 196	3^3	= 27
4^2	= 16	15^2	= 225	4^3	= 64
5^2	= 25			5^3	= 125
6^2	= 36				
7^2	= 49				
8^2	= 64				
9^2	= 81				
10^2	= 100				
11^2	= 121				

PRACTICE SET 17

Simplify each of the following:

1. 2^2

2. 2^3

3. 7^0

4. 3^2

5. 3^3

6. 10^4

7. $\left(\dfrac{1}{4}\right)^3$

8. $\left(\dfrac{4}{5}\right)^2$

9. $(-2)^2$

10. $(-2)^3$

11. -2^2

12. 8^2

13. 4^3

14. $(5^2)^2$

15. $(3^2)(3^3)$

16. $(x^3)(x^7)$

17. $\dfrac{8^5}{8^3}$

18. $\dfrac{8^3}{8^5}$

19. $\dfrac{x^7}{x^3}$

20. $\dfrac{4^{(n+1)}}{4^n}$

Which term is greater?

21. $(-3)^2$ or $(-3)^3$

22. 10^2 or 2^{10}

23. $\left(\dfrac{1}{2}\right)^2$ or $\left(\dfrac{1}{2}\right)^3$

24. 0.1 or 0.1^2

25. $(-5)^2$ or -5^2

ANSWERS AND EXPLANATIONS—PRACTICE SET 17

1. 4 $2^2 = 2 \times 2 = 4$

2. 8 $2^3 = 2 \times 2 \times 2 = 8$

3. 1 $7^0 = 1$ (A non-zero number raised to the 0 power equals 1.)

4. 9 $3^2 = 3 \times 3 = 9$

5. 27 $3^3 = 3 \times 3 \times 3 = 27$

6. 10,000 $10^4 = 10,000$ (The exponent tells you how many zeros you need.)

7. $\dfrac{1}{64}$ $\left(\dfrac{1}{4}\right)^3 = \dfrac{1}{4} \times \dfrac{1}{4} \times \dfrac{1}{4} = \dfrac{1}{64}$

8. $\dfrac{16}{25}$ $\left(\dfrac{4}{5}\right)^2 = \dfrac{4}{5} \times \dfrac{4}{5} = \dfrac{16}{25}$

9. 4 $(-2)^2 = -2 \times -2 = 4$

10. -8 $(-2)^3 = -2 \times -2 \times -2 = -8$

11. -4 $-2^2 = -(2)(2) = -4$ (If this seems counterintuitive, think of the problem $1 - 2^2$, which is equal to $1 - 4$ rather than $1 + 4$.)

12. 64 $8^2 = 8 \times 8 = 64$

13. 64 $4^3 = 4 \times 4 \times 4 = 64$

14. 625 $\left(5^2\right)^2 = 5^{2 \times 2} = 5^4 = 5 \times 5 \times 5 \times 5 = 625$

15. 243 $\left(3^2\right)\left(3^3\right) = 3^{2+3} = 3^5 = 3 \times 3 \times 3 \times 3 \times 3 = 243$

16. x^{10} $\left(x^3\right)\left(x^7\right) = x^{3+7} = x^{10}$

17. 64 $\dfrac{8^5}{8^3} = 8^{5-3} = 8^2 = 8 \times 8 = 64$

18. $\dfrac{1}{64}$ $\dfrac{8^3}{8^5} = 8^{3-5} = 8^{-2} = \dfrac{1}{8^2} = \dfrac{1}{8 \times 8} = \dfrac{1}{64}$

19. x^4 $\dfrac{x^7}{x^3} = x^{7-3} = x^4$

20. 4 $\dfrac{4^{(n+1)}}{4^n} = 4^{(n+1)-n} = 4^{n+1-n} = 4^1 = 4$

21. $(-3)^2$ $(-3)^2$ is a positive number and $(-3)^3$ is a negative number:

       $(-3)^2 = (-3)(-3) = 9$

       $(-3)^3 = (-3)(-3)(-3) = -27$

22. 2^{10} $10^2 = 100$ and

       $2^{10} = (2 \times 2 \times 2 \times 2 \times 2)(2 \times 2 \times 2 \times 2 \times 2)$

           $= 32 \times 32$ $\leftarrow$ (clearly 2^{10} is greater)

           $= 1024$

23. $\left(\dfrac{1}{2}\right)^2$ Since we have the same fraction, we can compare exponents. The fraction with the smaller exponent is greater:

       $\left(\dfrac{1}{2}\right)^2 = \dfrac{1}{2} \times \dfrac{1}{2} = \dfrac{1}{4}$

       $\left(\dfrac{1}{2}\right)^3 = \dfrac{1}{2} \times \dfrac{1}{2} \times \dfrac{1}{2} = \dfrac{1}{8}$

       Note that this method works only with fractions or decimals between 0 and 1 raised to positive powers.

24. 0.1   Since we have the same decimal fraction, we can compare exponents. The decimal fraction with the smaller exponent is greater:

       $0.1^{(1)} = 0.1$

       $0.1^{(2)} = .1 \times .1 = .01$

       Note that this method works only with fractions or decimals between 0 and 1 raised to positive powers.

25. $(-5)^2$ $(-5)^2$ is a positive number and -5^2 is a negative number:

       $(-5)^2 = (-5)(-5) = 25$

       $-5^2 = -(5)(5) = -25$

Roots

Roots Defined

Recall that fractional exponents denote *roots*. A root is a number that when taken as a factor a specified number of times gives a certain number. $9^{\frac{1}{2}} = \sqrt{9} = 3$. 3 is the *square* root of 9, because the square of 3 equals 9 ($3^2 = 9$). The radical sign ($\sqrt{\ }$) without a number in the pocket always denotes the square root. A cubed root is denoted $\sqrt[3]{\ }$, because a "3" exists in the pocket of the radical. A fifth root would be denoted with a "5" in the pocket $\left(\sqrt[5]{\ }\right)$. Here are a few examples to illustrate these relationships:

$$32^{\frac{1}{5}} = \sqrt[5]{32} = \sqrt[5]{2 \times 2 \times 2 \times 2 \times 2} = 2$$
$$16^{\frac{1}{4}} = \sqrt[4]{16} = \sqrt[4]{2 \times 2 \times 2 \times 2} = 2$$
$$8^{\frac{1}{3}} = \sqrt[3]{8} = \sqrt[3]{2 \times 2 \times 2} = 2$$
$$4^{\frac{1}{2}} = \sqrt{4} = \sqrt{2 \times 2} = 2$$

Approximation and Simplification of Roots

Numbers whose square roots are whole numbers, such as 1, 4, 9, 16, 25, 36, 49, 64, 81, and 100 are called *perfect squares*. Numbers such as 8, 27, 64, and 125 are called *perfect cubes*. Square and cubed roots oftentimes aren't whole numbers and must be *approximated*.

It would be a good idea to remember these square root approximations:

$\sqrt{2} \approx 1.4$

$\sqrt{3} \approx 1.7$

$\sqrt{5} \approx 2.2$

To simplify square roots:

(1) Write the square root of a number as the product of the square roots of that number's factors: $\sqrt{xy} = \sqrt{x} \times \sqrt{y}$

(2) Write the square root of a fraction as the square root of one number (the numerator) divided by the square root of another number (the denominator): $\sqrt{\dfrac{x}{y}} = \dfrac{\sqrt{x}}{\sqrt{y}}$

Here are a few examples:

$$\sqrt{135} = \sqrt{9} \times \sqrt{15} = 3\sqrt{15}$$

$$\sqrt{1,800} = \sqrt{900} \times \sqrt{2} = 30\sqrt{2}$$

$$\sqrt{\frac{9}{4}} = \frac{\sqrt{9}}{\sqrt{4}} = \frac{3}{2}$$

Operations with Roots

You can add and subtract expressions containing roots, *only* if the roots taken are the same; and you add and subtract only the numbers *outside* the radicals:

$$2\sqrt{3} - 10\sqrt{3} = -8\sqrt{3}$$

$8\sqrt{6} + \sqrt{6} = 9\sqrt{6}$ (no number in front of a radical implies a "1")

$$6\sqrt{16} + 8\sqrt{16} = 14\sqrt{16} = 14\sqrt{4 \times 4} = 14(4) = 56$$

$$10\sqrt{5} + 3\sqrt{45} = 10\sqrt{5} + 3\sqrt{9 \times 5} = 10\sqrt{5} + 3\sqrt{3 \times 3 \times 5} = 10\sqrt{5} + 3(3)\sqrt{5} = 10\sqrt{5} + 9\sqrt{5} = 19\sqrt{5}$$

$$6\sqrt{2} - 5\sqrt{4} = 6\sqrt{2} - 5\sqrt{2 \times 2} = 6\sqrt{2} - 5(2) = 6\sqrt{2} - 10$$

Sample Question 26: What is $2\sqrt{2} + 8\sqrt{2} + 9\sqrt{4} - 7\sqrt{16} - 3\sqrt{8}$?

Process (words)	Process (numbers)
(1) simplify terms	$9\sqrt{4} = 9\sqrt{2 \times 2} = 9(2) = 18$ $7\sqrt{16} = 7\sqrt{4 \times 4} = 7(4) = 28$ $3\sqrt{8} = 3\sqrt{4 \times 2} = 3\sqrt{2 \times 2 \times 2} = 3(2)\sqrt{2} = 6\sqrt{2}$
(2) plug in simplified terms	(2) $2\sqrt{2} + 8\sqrt{2} + 18 - 28 - 6\sqrt{2}$
(3) combine like terms	(3) $4\sqrt{2} - 10$
(4) approximate value if needed	(4) $4(1.4) - 10 = 5.6 - 10 = -4.4$

You can multiply and divide expressions containing roots, regardless of whether or not the roots taken are the same; and you multiply or divide both the numbers *inside* the radicals, and those *outside*:

$$64\sqrt{4} \div 8\sqrt{2} = 8\sqrt{2}$$

$$525\sqrt{222} \div 5\sqrt{111} = 105\sqrt{2}$$

$$\sqrt{8} \times 2\sqrt{3} = 2\sqrt{24} = 2\sqrt{6 \times 4} = 4\sqrt{6}$$

$$\sqrt{25} \div 25 = 5 \div 25 = \frac{5}{25} = \frac{1}{5}$$

$$16 \div \sqrt{16} = 16 \div 4 = 4$$

Sample Question 27:   What is $8\sqrt{2} \times 6\sqrt{2} \times 30\sqrt{4} \div 8\sqrt{4}$?

Process (words)	Process (numbers)
(1) multiply/divide terms outside radicals	(1) $8 \times 6 \times 30 \div 8$ $= 48 \times 30 \div 8$ $= 1,440 \div 8$ $= 180$
(2) multiply/divide terms inside radicals	(2) $2 \times 2 \times 4 \div 4$ $= 16 \div 4$ $= 4$
(3) combine the two products on either side of radical	(3) $180\sqrt{4}$
(4) simplify the expression	$= 180\sqrt{2 \times 2}$ $= 180(2)$ $= 360$

Squaring square roots is easy as it gives you the number already there:

$$\left(\sqrt{32}\right)^2 = 32$$

$$\left(8\sqrt{16}\right)^2 = 8^2 \times 16 = 64 \times 16 = 1,024$$

PRACTICE SET 18

Simplify each of the following:

1. $\sqrt{25}$

2. $\sqrt{4}$

3. $\sqrt{49}$

4. $\sqrt{64}$

5. $\sqrt[3]{64}$

6. $\sqrt[6]{64}$

7. $\sqrt{9}\sqrt{4}$

8. $\sqrt{\frac{25}{16}}$

9. $\sqrt[4]{\frac{81}{16}}$

10. $3\sqrt{2} + 4\sqrt{2}$

11. $7\sqrt{2} + 3\sqrt{3} - 2\sqrt{2} + 4\sqrt{3}$

12. $\sqrt{2} + 2\sqrt{18}$

13. $\dfrac{\sqrt{32}}{\sqrt{48}}$

14. $\dfrac{2\sqrt{27} - 3\sqrt{3}}{2\sqrt{3}}$

15. $\sqrt{2}\left(3\sqrt{2} + 4\sqrt{8}\right)$

112

ANSWERS AND EXPLANATIONS—PRACTICE SET 18

1. 5 $\sqrt{25} = \sqrt{5 \times 5} = 5$

2. 2 $\sqrt{4} = \sqrt{2 \times 2} = 2$

3. 7 $\sqrt{49} = \sqrt{7 \times 7} = 7$

4. 8 $\sqrt{64} = \sqrt{8 \times 8} = 8$

5. 4 $\sqrt[3]{64} = \sqrt[3]{4 \times 4 \times 4} = 4$

6. 2 $\sqrt[6]{64} = \sqrt[6]{4 \times 4 \times 4} = \sqrt[6]{2 \times 2 \times 2 \times 2 \times 2 \times 2} = 2$

7. 6 $\sqrt{9}\sqrt{4} = \sqrt{36} = \sqrt{6 \times 6} = 6$

8. $\frac{5}{4}$ $\sqrt{\frac{25}{16}} = \sqrt{\frac{5 \times 5}{4 \times 4}} = \frac{5}{4}$

9. $\frac{3}{2}$ $\sqrt[4]{\frac{81}{16}} = \sqrt[4]{\frac{9 \times 9}{4 \times 4}} = \sqrt[4]{\frac{3 \times 3 \times 3 \times 3}{2 \times 2 \times 2 \times 2}} = \frac{3}{2}$

10. $7\sqrt{2}$ $3\sqrt{2} + 4\sqrt{2} = (3+4)\sqrt{2} = 7\sqrt{2}$

11. $5\sqrt{2} + 7\sqrt{3}$ $7\sqrt{2} + 3\sqrt{3} - 2\sqrt{2} + 4\sqrt{3} = \left(7\sqrt{2} - 2\sqrt{2}\right) + \left(3\sqrt{3} + 4\sqrt{3}\right) = 5\sqrt{2} + 7\sqrt{3}$

12. $7\sqrt{2}$ $\sqrt{2} + 2\sqrt{18} = \sqrt{2} + 2\sqrt{3 \times 3 \times 2} = \sqrt{2} + 2(3)\sqrt{2} = \sqrt{2} + 6\sqrt{2} = 7\sqrt{2}$

13. $\frac{\sqrt{2}}{\sqrt{3}}$ or $\frac{\sqrt{6}}{3}$ $\frac{\sqrt{32}}{\sqrt{48}} = \frac{\sqrt{16 \times 2}}{\sqrt{16 \times 3}} = \frac{4\sqrt{2}}{4\sqrt{3}} = \frac{\sqrt{2}}{\sqrt{3}} = \frac{\sqrt{2}}{\sqrt{3}}\frac{\sqrt{3}}{\sqrt{3}} = \frac{\sqrt{6}}{3}$

14. $\frac{3}{2}$ $\frac{2\sqrt{27} - 3\sqrt{3}}{2\sqrt{3}} = \frac{2\sqrt{9 \times 3} - 3\sqrt{3}}{2\sqrt{3}} = \frac{2(3)\sqrt{3} - 3\sqrt{3}}{2\sqrt{3}} = \frac{6\sqrt{3} - 3\sqrt{3}}{2\sqrt{3}} = \frac{3\sqrt{3}}{2\sqrt{3}} = \frac{3}{2}$

15. 22 $\sqrt{2}\left(3\sqrt{2} + 4\sqrt{8}\right) = 3\sqrt{2 \times 2} + 4\sqrt{8 \times 2} = 3(2) + 4(4) = 6 + 16 = 22$

Order of Operations

The Order

Now that you've reviewed exponents and roots, further practice simplifying complex expressions is in order. Recall the PEMDAS mnemonic (Please Excuse My Dear Aunt Sally). Remember that P stands for parentheses, E stands for exponents, M stands for multiplication, D stands for division, A stands for addition, and S stands for subtraction.

The Operations

Multiplication and addition are both *commutative*; that is, the operation(s) can be performed in any order: $8 \times 9 = 9 \times 8$ and $8 + 9 = 9 + 8$, and *associative*; that is, the operation(s) can be regrouped in any order: $5 \times (3 \times 15) = (5 \times 3) \times 15$ and $8 + (102 + 25) + 75 = (8 + 102) + (25 + 75)$.

Multiplication and division are *distributive*; that is, factors and divisors can be distributed across terms being added or subtracted: $8(1 + 9) = 8 + 72$ and $8(1 - 9) = 8 - 72$ and $\frac{(8+2)}{6} = \frac{8}{6} + \frac{2}{6}$ and $\frac{(8-2)}{6} = \frac{8}{6} - \frac{2}{6}$.

Sample Question 28: What is $(3 \times 5)^2 + \sqrt{121} \times (3+6) - 18 \times 2 + 11\sqrt{400}$?

Process (words)	Process (numbers)
(1) get rid of parentheses	(1) $15^2 + \sqrt{121} \times 9 - 18 \times 2 + 11\sqrt{400}$
(2) simplify exponents/radicals	(2) $225 + 11 \times 9 - 18 \times 2 + 11(20)$
(3) multiply and divide from left	(3) $225 + 99 - 36 + 220$
(4) add and subtract from left	(4) $324 - 36 + 220$ $= 288 + 220$ $= 508$

Sample Question 29: What is $512^{\frac{1}{3}} + 3\sqrt{3} + \frac{8}{\sqrt{9}} + 21 \div \frac{\sqrt{49}}{2\sqrt{81}}$?

Process (words)	Process (numbers)
(1) get rid of parentheses	(1) not applicable
(2) simplify exponents/radicals	(2) $8 + 3\sqrt{3} + \frac{8}{3} + 21 \div \frac{7}{18}$

(3) multiply and divide from left	(3) $8+3\sqrt{3}+\dfrac{8}{3}+21\times\dfrac{18}{7}$
	$=8+3\sqrt{3}+\dfrac{8}{3}+\dfrac{3}{1}\times\dfrac{18}{1}$
	$=8+3\sqrt{3}+\dfrac{8}{3}+54$
(4) add and subtract from left	(4) $64\dfrac{2}{3}+3\sqrt{3}$

Sample Question 30: What is $6(3-2)+3(18-16)\times 3+2^{-3}$?

Process (words)	Process (numbers)
(1) get rid of parentheses	(1) $6(1)+3(2)\times 3+2^{-3}$
(2) simplify exponents/radicals	(2) $6(1)+3(2)\times 3+\dfrac{1}{2}\times\dfrac{1}{2}\times\dfrac{1}{2}$
(3) multiply and divide from left	(3) $6+18+\dfrac{1}{8}$
(4) add and subtract from left	(4) $24\dfrac{1}{8}$

Sample Question 31: What is $\sqrt{4}(2-3)+\sqrt{2}-3\sqrt{2}+\left(3^4+2\right)$?

Process (words)	Process (numbers)
(1) get rid of parentheses	(1) $\sqrt{4}(-1)+\sqrt{2}-3\sqrt{2}+83$
(2) simplify exponents/radicals	(2) $2(-1)+\sqrt{2}-3\sqrt{2}+83$
(3) multiply and divide from left	(3) $-2+\sqrt{2}-3\sqrt{2}+83$
(4) add and subtract from left	(4) $81-2\sqrt{2}$

PRACTICE SET 19

1. $\sqrt{4^2 + 3^2}$

2. $4^2(6+8)$

3. $-(11-9)+(7^2-40)$

4. $(5(6-8))^2$

5. $(5-6)^2-(6-5)$

6. $4(\sqrt{16}+\sqrt{9})^{-2}+\dfrac{3}{(10-3)^2}$

7. $\sqrt{2}(3\sqrt{18}-2\sqrt{18})+100^{\frac{1}{2}}$

8. $2((\sqrt{4}+\sqrt{8})-2(1+\sqrt{8}))^2$

9. $(3(6-4)+2(5-2))^2+((6-3)^2-7)^2$

10. $\sqrt{2}(\sqrt{8}+\sqrt{32})\div(\sqrt{8})^2$

ANSWERS AND EXPLANATIONS—PRACTICE SET 19

1. 5

$$\sqrt{4^2 + 3^2} = \sqrt{16 + 9}$$
$$= \sqrt{25}$$
$$= 5$$

2. 224

$$4^2(6 + 8) = 16(14)$$
$$= 224$$

3. 7

$$-(11 - 9) + (7^2 - 40) = -(2) + (49 - 40)$$
$$= -2 + 9$$
$$= 7$$

4. 100

$$(5(6 - 8))^2 = (5(-2))^2$$
$$= (-10)^2$$
$$= 100$$

5. 0

$$(5 - 6)^2 - (6 - 5) = (-1)^2 - 1$$
$$= 1 - 1$$
$$= 0$$

6. $\dfrac{1}{7}$

$$4\left(\sqrt{16}+\sqrt{9}\right)^{-2}+\dfrac{3}{(10-3)^2}=4(4+3)^{-2}+\dfrac{3}{(7)^2}$$

$$=4(7)^{-2}+\dfrac{3}{49}$$

$$=4\left(\dfrac{1}{7^2}\right)+\dfrac{3}{49}$$

$$=4\left(\dfrac{1}{49}\right)+\dfrac{3}{49}$$

$$=\dfrac{4}{49}+\dfrac{3}{49}$$

$$=\dfrac{7}{49}$$

$$=\dfrac{1}{7}$$

7. 16

$$\sqrt{2}\left(3\sqrt{18}-2\sqrt{18}\right)+100^{\frac{1}{2}}=\sqrt{2}\left(\sqrt{18}\right)+\sqrt{100}$$

$$=\sqrt{36}+\sqrt{100}$$

$$=6+10$$

$$=16$$

8. 16

$$2\left(\left(\sqrt{4}+\sqrt{8}\right)-2\left(1+\sqrt{8}\right)\right)^2=2\left(\left(2+\sqrt{8}\right)-2-2\sqrt{8}\right)^2$$

$$=2\left(-\sqrt{8}\right)^2$$

$$=2(8)$$

$$=16$$

9. 36

$$\left(3(6-4)+2(5-2)\right)^2 + \left((6-3)^2 - 7\right)^2 = \frac{\left(3(2)+2(3)\right)^2}{\left((3)^2 - 7\right)^2}$$

$$= \frac{(6+6)^2}{(9-7)^2}$$

$$= \frac{12^2}{2^2}$$

$$= \frac{6^2 2^2}{2^2}$$

$$= 6^2$$

$$= 36$$

10. $\dfrac{3}{2}$

$$\sqrt{2}\left(\sqrt{8} + \sqrt{32}\right) + \left(\sqrt{8}\right)^2 = \frac{\sqrt{16} + \sqrt{64}}{8}$$

$$= \frac{4+8}{8}$$

$$= \frac{12}{8}$$

$$= \frac{3}{2}$$

Algebraic Expressions

Terms

Algebraic expressions are expressions that include unknowns or *variables*. $3xy$ is an algebraic expression. $3xy$ reads as 3 times x times y. The variables are x and y, and 3 is the *coefficient*. In the absence of a visible coefficient, a coefficient of 1 is understood: $xy = 1xy$. Plus and minus signs separate terms, so the expression $3xy + 2xy - 8 + 2x^2$ contains 4 terms. Because they contain only one term, expressions such as $3xy$ and xy are known as *monomials*. $3xy - 1$ is a *polynomial* as are all expressions that have two or more terms. (These are the common usages of these words. Technically, all monomials are a type of polynomial.) Because the variables in algebraic expressions always stand for a number, you can treat algebraic expressions as you do numerical expressions.

Evaluating Algebraic Expressions

Evaluating an algebraic expression involves substituting in given numbers for one or more of the unknowns in the expression. Side by side variables indicate multiplication, but side by side numbers indicate a new number, so, to avoid mistakes, enclose in parentheses the number[s] given for substitution:

If $x = -2$ and $y = 2$, what's the value of $2xy + x - xy$?

$$= 2(-2)(2) + (-2) - (-2)(2)$$
$$= -8 - 2 + 4$$
$$= -10 + 4$$
$$= -6$$

Sample Question 32: What is the value of $3xy$ if $x = -2$ and $y = \frac{2}{3}$?

Process (words)	Process (numbers)
(1) substitute in given values	(1) $3(-2)(\frac{2}{3})$
(2) perform the operations according to PEMDAS	(2) $-6(\frac{2}{3})$ $= -\frac{12}{3}$ $= -4$

Sample Question 33: If $x = -1$ and $y = 3$, what is the value of $x^7 + y - (3x + 2y^2)$?

Process (words)	Process (numbers)
(1) substitute in given values	(1) $(-1)^7 + 3 - (3(-1) + 2(3)^2)$
(2) perform the operations according to PEMDAS	(2) $(-1)^7 + 3 - (-3 + 2(9))$ $= -1 + 3 - (-3 + 2(9))$ $= -1 + 3 - (-3 + 18)$ $= -1 + 3 - (15)$ $= -1 + 3 - 15$ $= 2 - 15$ $= -13$

Addition and Subtraction of Algebraic Expressions

Add and subtract *like* algebraic expressions by adding and subtracting their coefficients (no coefficient means "1"). Like expressions are those that have the same variables raised to the same powers: xyz^2 and $14xyz^2$ are like terms but x^2yz and $14x^2yz^2$ are not like terms. Unlike terms *cannot* be combined:

$3x + 2y = 3x + 2y$

$3x + 2xy + 4x = 7x + 2xy$

$3xy + 2x + 3y + 4y + 6xy + 2x - x = (3xy + 6xy) + (3y + 4y) + (2x + 2x - x) = 9xy + 7y + 3x$

Multiplication of Algebraic Expressions

Multiply *like* and *unlike* algebraic expressions by multiplying the coefficients and variables independently.

Here are four things to remember about multiplying algebraic expressions:

1. To multiply a monomial by a monomial, multiply the coefficients and then multiply the variables by adding the exponents of the like variables:

    $(3xy)(3xyz) = 9x^2y^2z$

2. To multiply a monomial by a polynomial, use the distributive law of multiplication:

    $y^2(y^2 + 2) = y^4 + 2y^2$

3. To multiply a binomial (2-termed expression) by a binomial use the FOIL (First, Outer, Inner, Last) method:

    $(3x + 6)(x + 5) =$

    multiply First terms: $3x \times x = 3x^2$
    multiply Outer terms: $3x \times 5 = 15x$
    multiply Inner terms: $6 \times x = 6x$
    multiply Last terms: $6 \times 5 = 30$
    add the products: $3x^2 + 21x + 30$

4. To multiply more than two expressions at a time, multiply the first two and then multiply the resulting product times the next expression and so on:

    $(x - 5)(3x + 2)(8x) =$

    $(x - 5)(3x + 2) = 3x^2 + 2x - 15x - 10 = 3x^2 - 13x - 10$ ←   (FOIL)

    $(8x)(3x^2 - 13x - 10) = 24x^3 - 104x^2 - 80x$ ←   (Distributive)

Division of Algebraic Expressions

Divide like and unlike monomial expressions by dividing the coefficients and the variables independently.

Here are two things to remember about dividing algebraic expressions:

1. To divide a monomial by a monomial, divide the coefficients and then divide the variables by subtracting:

$$21x^2y^4 \div 3xy = 7x^{2-1}y^{4-1} = 7x^1y^3 = 7xy^3$$

2. To divide a polynomial by a monomial, use the distributive law of division:

$$\frac{3xy + 2x^2y^2 + y^{-2}}{xy} = \frac{3xy}{xy} + \frac{2x^2y^2}{xy} + \frac{y^{-2}}{xy}$$

$$= 3 + 2xy + \frac{\left(\frac{1}{y}\right)^2}{xy}$$

$$= 3 + 2xy + \frac{1}{y^2} \times \frac{1}{xy}$$

$$= 3 + 2xy + \frac{1}{xy^3}$$

Simplifying Algebraic Expressions

Simplifying algebraic expressions is necessary to solving complex problems. You can simplify algebraic expressions just as you would numerical expressions (in accordance with PEMDAS). (Remember to combine any like terms.)

$8xy^2 \div 8xy^2$ simplifies to 1

$\dfrac{14a^2b^3c^4}{28a^4b^2c}$ simplifies to $\dfrac{bc^3}{2a^2}$

$\dfrac{25x^3y^3z^3}{75x^2y^4z}$ simplifies to $\dfrac{xz^2}{3y}$

$x^2y + (x)(xy) + 3z - 10z + x^2(5y)$ simplifies to $7x^2y - 7z$

PRACTICE SET 20

Solve the equations by substituting the variables with the given value:

1. $2x + 8$ $x = 3$

2. $x^2 + x^3$ $x = -2$

3. $a^{-3} + b^{-3}$ $a = 2, b = \dfrac{1}{2}$

4. $x^2 + 2xy + y^2$ $x = 4, y = -4$

5. $3ab + 2(a - b)^2 - c$ $a = 3, b = 4, c = 20$

Perform the following multiplications and divisions:

6. $6y(x + 2y)$

7. $2mn(2m + 3n)$

8. $xyz\left(x + xy^2 + z^3\right)$

9. $(x + 2)(x - 7)$

10. $(2x + 3)(x + 4)$

11. $(x - 5)(x - 5)$

12. $(x + 2)(x - 2)(x + 5)$

13. $\dfrac{xy}{x}$

14. $\dfrac{3x^2y^3}{2x}$

15. $\dfrac{14a^3b^2c}{35ab^2c^3}$

124

ANSWERS AND EXPLANATIONS—PRACTICE SET 20

1. 14

$$2x + 8 = 2(3) + 8$$
$$= 6 + 8$$
$$= 14$$

2. −4

$$x^2 + x^3 = (-2)^2 + (-2)^3$$
$$= 4 - 8$$
$$= -4$$

3. $\dfrac{65}{8}$ or $8\dfrac{1}{8}$

$$a^{-3} + b^{-3} = \frac{1}{a^3} + \frac{1}{b^3}$$
$$= \frac{1}{2^3} + \frac{1}{\frac{1}{2}^3}$$
$$= \frac{1}{8} + \frac{1}{\frac{1}{8}}$$
$$= \frac{1}{8} + 8 \leftarrow \left(\text{to get the 8:} \quad \frac{1}{\frac{1}{8}} = 1 \div \tfrac{1}{8} = 1 \times \tfrac{8}{1} = 8 \right)$$
$$= 8\frac{1}{8}$$

4. 0

$$x^2 + 2xy + y^2 = (4)^2 + 2(4)(-4) + (-4)^2$$
$$= 16 - 32 + 16$$
$$= 0$$

5. 18

$$3ab + 2(a - b)^2 - c = 3(3)(4) + 2(3 - 4)^2 - 20$$
$$= 36 + 2(-1)^2 - 20$$
$$= 36 + 2 - 20$$
$$= 18$$

6. $6xy + 12y^2$

$$6y(x + 2y) = 6y(x) + 6y(2y)$$
$$= 6xy + 12y^2$$

7. $4m^2n + 6mn^2$

$$2mn(2m + 3n) = 2mn(2m) + 2mn(3n)$$
$$= 4m^2n + 6mn^2$$

8. $x^2yz + x^2y^3z + xyz^4$

$$xyz(x + xy^2 + z^3) = xyz(x) + xyz(xy^2) + xyz(z^3)$$
$$= x^2yz + x^2y^3z + xyz^4$$

9. $x^2 - 5x - 14$

$$(x + 2)(x - 7) = x(x) - 7(x) + 2(x) + 2(-7) \leftarrow \text{use FOIL}$$
$$= x^2 - 5x - 14 \leftarrow \text{combine like terms}$$

10. $2x^2 + 11x + 12$

$$(2x + 3)(x + 4) = 2x(x) + 4(2x) + 3(x) + 3(4) \leftarrow \text{use FOIL}$$
$$= 2x^2 + 11x + 12 \leftarrow \text{combine like terms}$$

11. $x^2 - 10x + 25$

$$(x - 5)(x - 5) = x(x) - 5(x) - 5(x) - 5(-5) \leftarrow \text{use FOIL}$$
$$= x^2 - 10x + 25 \leftarrow \text{combine like terms}$$

12. $x^3 + 5x^2 - 4x - 20$

$$(x + 2)(x - 2)(x + 5) = x^2 - 2x + 2x - 4(x + 5) \leftarrow \text{FOIL first two terms}$$
$$= (x^2 - 4)(x + 5) \leftarrow \text{combine like terms}$$
$$= x^3 + 5x^2 - 4x - 20 \leftarrow \text{use FOIL}$$

13. y

$$\frac{xy}{x} = y \leftarrow \text{eliminate one } x \text{ in both halves}$$

14. $\dfrac{3xy^3}{2}$ or $\dfrac{3}{2}xy^3$

$\dfrac{3x^2y^3}{2x} = \dfrac{3xy^3}{2}$ or $\dfrac{3}{2}xy^3$ ← eliminate one x in both halves

15. $\dfrac{2a^2}{5c^2}$

$\dfrac{14a^3b^2c}{35ab^2c^3} = \dfrac{2a^2}{5c^2}$ ← eliminate $7ab^2c$ from both halves

Factoring Expressions

Factoring out Common Monomials

Use the reverse of the distributive law to factor out common monomials:

$6xy + 12x + 3y = 3(2xy + 4x + y)$

If a particular variable appears in every term of an expression, it can be factored out by dividing each term by the particular variable raised to the lowest power it has in any of the terms.

$x^2 + x^3y = x^2(1 + xy)$

$3xy + 6x^2y + 6xy^2 = 3xy(1 + 2x + 2y) = 3xy(2y + 2x + 1)$

Factoring the Difference of Two Squares

Binomials of the form $a^2 - b^2$ factor into two linear, or first degree binomial factors. The terms in one of the factors are subtracted, and the terms in the other are added. Our example $a^2 - b^2$, factors to $(a - b)(a + b)$. Always keep the roots on the sides of the equation that their squares appear on:

$9x^2 - 4y^2 = (3x)^2 - (2y)^2 = (3x - 2y)(3x + 2y)$

Other difference of two squares binomials factor in the same way, though the resulting factors are not always linear:

$16x^2y^4 - 121z^2 = (4xy^2)^2 - (11z)^2 = (4xy^2 - 11z)(4xy^2 + 11z)$

Factoring Classic Trinomials

Trinomials of the form $ax^2 + bx + c$ can sometimes be factored into two linear binomials. A reverse of the FOIL method can be used to determine the terms in the factors. The first terms of the factors must multiply to the first term of the trinomial, the last terms of the factors must multiply to the last term of the trinomial, and the products of the inner and outer terms of the binomials must sum to the middle term of the trinomial. Factoring these kinds of trinomials requires a little bit of trial and error:

$x^2 - 6x + 8 = (x - 4)(x - 2)$

$x^2 - 3x - 18 = (x + 3)(x - 6)$

$x^2 + 2x - 24 = (x - 4)(x + 6)$

Trinomials of the form $a^2 + 2ab + b^2$ factor into two identical binomials. In each, the first term is made up of the square root of the first term of the trinomial and the second term is made up of the square root of the last term of the trinomial. The two terms are separated by an addition sign. Our example $a^2 + 2ab + b^2$, factors to $(a + b)(a + b)$, or $(a + b)^2$. Here are a few examples:

$x^2 + 8x + 16 = (x + 4)(x + 4) = (x + 4)^2$

$x^2 + 10x + 25 = (x + 5)(x + 5) = (x + 5)^2$

$x^2 + 12x + 36 = (x + 6)(x + 6) + (x + 6)^2$

Sample Question 34: Factor $2x^2 + 12x + 18$.

Process (words)	Process (numbers)
(1) factor out the common monomial factor	(1) $2(x^2 + 6x + 9)$
(2) write the first term of the trinomial as the first factors of the binomials	(2) $2(x\ \ )(x\ \ )$
(3) write the pairs of numbers whose product is 9	(3) 1 and 9 or -1 and -9 3 and 3 or -3 and -3
(4) determine which of the pairs sum to +6	(4) 3 and 3
(5) fill in the pair picked	(5) $2(x + 3)(x + 3)$
(6) check your answer by multiplying the first two terms	(6) $2(x + 3) = 2x + 6$

(7) and the product of the first two by the third (use FOIL)

(7) $(2x + 6)(x + 3)$

multiply first terms	$2x \times x = 2x^2$
multiply outer terms	$2x \times 3 = 6x$
multiply inner terms	$6 \times x = 6x$
multiply last terms	$6 \times 3 = 18$
add the products	$2x^2 + 12x + 18$

PRACTICE SET 21

Factor the following expressions:

1. $3a + 6b + 18c$

2. $9x^2y + 27xy^2$

3. $24r^2st + 6r^2s + 3r^4t$

4. $x^2 - y^2$

5. $4x^2 - 9y^2$

6. $16a^4 - 9b^2c^2$

7. $a^2 - 4$

8. $m^2 - 1$

9. $x^2 + 2x + 1$

10. $x^2 + 8x + 12$

11. $x^2 - 8x + 12$

12. $x^2 - 4x - 12$

13. $x^2 + 4x - 12$

14. $4z^2 + 5z + 1$

15. $4y^2 - 3y - 1$

16. $m^2 - 10m + 25$

17. $x^2 + 4xy + 4y^2$

18. $2mn^2 + 8mn + 6m$

19. $x^2y^2z^2 + 4xy^3z^2 + 3y^4z^2$

20. $27m^2n^2 - 12m^4$

When factoring trinomials into binomials, the second sign (i.e., + or –) in the trinomial is helpful to determine the signs of the binomials. If the *second* sign is +, then *both* of the binomial signs will be the same as the *first* sign in the trinomial. For instance, in the expression $m^2 - 10m + 25$ the second sign is positive (+) and therefore *both* of the binomial expressions will have negative (–) signs.

If the second sign in the trinomial is negative, then one of the signs in the binomial will be positive, and one will be negative, but you don't know which is which.

ANSWERS AND EXPLANATIONS—PRACTICE SET 21

1. $3(a + 2b + 6c)$

   $3a + 6b + 18c = 3(a + 2b + 6c) \leftarrow$ factor a 3 out of each term

2. $9xy(x + 3y)$

   $9x^2y + 27xy^2 = 9xy(x + 3y) \leftarrow$ factor $9xy$ out of each term

3. $3r^2\left(8st + 2s + r^2t\right)$

   $24r^2st + 6r^2s + 3r^4t = 3r^2\left(8st + 2s + r^2t\right) \leftarrow$ factor $3r^2$ out of each term

4. $(x - y)\,(x + y)$

   $x^2 - y^2 = (x - y)(x + y) \leftarrow$ difference of two squares

5. $(2x - 3y)\,(2x + 3y)$

   $4x^2 - 9y^2 = (2x - 3y)(2x + 3y) \leftarrow$ difference of two squares

6. $\left(4a^2 - 3bc\right)\left(4a^2 + 3bc\right)$

   $16a^4 - 9b^2c^2 = \left(4a^2 - 3bc\right)\left(4a^2 + 3bc\right) \leftarrow$ difference of two squares

7. $(a - 2)\,(a + 2)$

   $a^2 - 4 = (a - 2)(a + 2) \leftarrow$ difference of two squares

8. $(m - 1)\,(m + 1)$

   $m^2 - 1 = (m - 1)(m + 2) \leftarrow$ difference of two squares

9. $(x + 1)^2$

   Write the first term of the trinomial as the first factors of the binomials:

   $x^2 + 2x + 1 = (x\quad)(x\quad)$

   List the pairs of numbers whose product is 1:

   1 and 1, -1 and -1

   Determine which pair sums to 2:

   1 and 1

Fill in the pair picked:

$(x+1)(x+1)$

10. $(x + 6) (x + 2)$

   Write the first term of the trinomial as the first factors of the binomials:

   $x^2 + 8x + 12 = (x \quad)(x \quad)$

   List the pairs of numbers whose product is 12:

   . 12 and 1, 4 and 3, 6 and 2 (and their negatives)

   Determine which pair sums to 8:

   6 and 2

   Fill in the pair picked:

   $(x+6)(x+2)$

11. $(x - 6) (x - 2)$

   Write the first term of the trinomial as the first factors of the binomials:

   $x^2 - 8x + 12 = (x \quad)(x \quad)$

   List the pairs of numbers whose product is 12:

   12 and 1, 4 and 3, 6 and 2 (and their negatives)

   Determine which pair sums to -8:

   -6 and -2

   Fill in the pair picked:

   $(x-6)(x-2)$

12. $(x - 6) (x + 2)$

   Write the first term of the trinomial as the first factors of the binomials:

   $x^2 - 4x - 12 = (x \quad)(x \quad)$

   List the pairs of numbers whose product is -12:

   12 and -1, 4 and -3, 6 and -2
   -12 and 1, -4 and 3, -6 and 2

Determine which pair sums to -4:

-6 and 2

Fill in the pair picked:

$(x-6)(x+2)$

13. $(x + 6)(x - 2)$

Write the first term of the trinomial as the first factors of the binomials:

$x^2 + 4x - 12 = (x\quad)(x\quad)$

List the pairs of numbers whose product is -12:

12 and -1, 4 and -3, 6 and -2
-12 and 1, -4 and 3, -6 and 2

Determine which pair sums to 4:

6 and -2

Fill in the pair picked:

$(x+6)(x-2)$

14. $(4z + 1)(z + 1)$

Write the first term of the trinomial as the first factors of the binomials:

$4z^2 + 5z + 1 = (4z\quad)(z\quad)$ or $(2z\quad)(2z\quad)$

List the pairs of numbers whose product is 1:

1 and 1, -1 and -1

Determine which pair, after multiplication by the coefficients of the possible first terms, sums to 5:

$4 \times 1 = 4$, $1 \times 1 = 1$ and $4 + 1 = 5$

Fill in the pair picked:

$(4z+1)(z+1)$

15. $(4y + 1)(y - 1)$

Write the first term of the trinomial as the first factors of the binomials:

$$4y^2 - 3y - 1 = (4y \quad)(y \quad) \text{ or } (2y \quad)(2y \quad)$$

List the pairs of numbers whose product is -1:

1 and -1

Determine which pair, after multiplication by the coefficients of the possible first terms, sums to -3:

$$4 \times -1 = -4, \ 1 \times 1 = 1 \text{ and } -4 + 1 = -3$$

Fill in the pair picked:

$$(4y + 1)(y - 1)$$

16. $(m - 5)^2$

Write the first term of the trinomial as the first factors of the binomials:

$$m^2 - 10m + 25 = (m \quad)(m \quad)$$

List the pairs of numbers whose product is 25:

1 and 25, 5 and 5 (and their negatives)

Determine which pair sums to -25:

-5 and -5

Fill in the pair picked:

$$(m - 5)(m - 5)$$

17. $(x + 2y)^2$

Write the first term of the trinomial as the first factors of the binomials:

$$x^2 + 4xy + 4y^2 = (x \quad)(x \quad)$$

List the pairs of numbers whose product is $4y^2$:

y and $4y$, $2y$ and $2y$ (and their negatives)

134

Determine which pair sums to $4y$:

$2y$ and $2y$

Fill in the pair picked:

$(x+2y)(x+2y)$

18. $2m(n+3)(n+1)$

$2mn^2 + 8mn + 6m$

Factor $2m$ out of each term:

$2m(n^2 + 4n + 3)$

Write the first term of the trinomial as the first factors of the binomials:

$n^2 + 4n + 3 = (n\quad)(n\quad)$

List the pairs of numbers whose product is 3:

3 and 1, -3 and -1

Determine which pair sums to 4:

3 and 1

Fill in the pair picked:

$2m(n+3)(n+1)$

19. $y^2z^2(x+3y)(x+y)$

$x^2y^2z^2 + 4x^2y^3z^2 + 3y^4z^2$

Factor y^2z^2 out of each term:

$y^2z^2(x^2 + 4xy + 3y^2)$

Write the first term of the trinomial as the first factors of the binomials:

$(x^2 + 4xy + 3y^2) = (x\quad)(x\quad)$

List the pairs of numbers whose product is $3y^2$:

$3y$ and y, $-3y$ and $-y$

Determine which of the pairs sums to $4y$:

$3y$ and y

Fill in the pair picked:

$y^2z^2(x+3y)(x+y)$

20. $3m^2(3n-2m)(3n+2m)$

$27m^2n^2 - 12m^4$

Factor $3m^2$ out of each term:

$3m^2(9n^2 - 4m^2)$
$3m^2(3n-2m)(3n+2m) \leftarrow$ difference of two squares

Equations

Linear Equations

Equal expressions form *equations*. A *linear* equation is one in which the variables are raised only to the first power (like x, not like x^2 or x^3). Since you can do most anything to one side of an equation, as long as you do it to the other side, solving linear equations is usually pretty simple.

To solve a linear equation:

(1) get the term or terms containing the variable on one side of the equation (this is usually done through addition and/or subtraction)
(2) get the variable entirely alone (this is usually done through multiplication and/or division)
(3) check your solution

In the examples that follow x is solved for and the solution is checked:

Example 1

$$20(x + 4) = 140$$
$$x + 4 = \frac{140}{20}$$
$$x + 4 = 7$$
$$x = 7 - 4$$
$$x = 3$$

Check your solution:

$$20(3 + 4) = 140$$
$$20(7) = 140$$
$$140 = 140$$

Example 2

$$\frac{2x}{5} = 300 - 6x + 20$$
$$2x = 5(300 - 6x + 20)$$
$$2x = 1500 - 30x + 100$$
$$2x + 30x = 1500 + 100$$
$$32x = 1600$$
$$x = \frac{1600}{32}$$
$$x = 50$$

Check your solution:

$$\frac{2(50)}{5} = 300 - 6(50) + 20$$

$$\frac{100}{5} = 300 - 300 + 20$$

$$20 = 20$$

The Zero Equations

You will encounter expressions which are set equal to, or can be set equal to, zero. It's important to remember that expressions set equal to zero *must* contain a factor of zero or they wouldn't be set equal to zero. If $xy = 0$, then either $x = 0$ or $y = 0$ or both x and $y = 0$.

To solve an equation set equal to zero:

(1) set each factor equal to zero
(2) solve each mini-equation
(3) check your solution[s]

In the examples that follow, x is solved for and the solution[s] are checked:

$x(x - 3) = 0$
$x = 0$ or $x = 3$
$0(0 - 3) = 0$ and $3(3 - 3) = 0$

$a (b + 3) = 0$
$a = 0$ or $b = -3$
$0(b + 3) = 0$ and $a (-3 + 3) = 0$

$(x - 2)(x + 2) = 0$
$x = 2$ or $x = -2$
$(2 - 2)(2 + 2) = 0$ and $(-2 - 2)(-2 + 2) = 0$

$(x + 4)(x + 4) = 0$
$x = -4$
$(-4 + 4)(-4 + 4) = 0$

$3xy (x) = 0$
$x = 0$ or $y = 0$
$3(0)y (0) = 0$ and $3x(0) (x) = 0$

$$\frac{(x-1)}{y} = 0$$

$$x = 1$$

$$\frac{1-1}{y} = 0 \quad (y \text{ cannot equal zero here because division by zero is impossible})$$

$$x^2 - 1 = 0$$

$$(x-1)(x+1) = 0$$

$$x = 1 \text{ or } x = -1$$

$$1^2 - 1 = 0 \text{ and } (-1)^2 - 1 = 0$$

Quadratic Equations

A *quadratic* equation is one in which variables are squared.

To solve quadratic equations:

(1) put the equation in standard form: $ax^2 + bx + c = 0$
(2) factor the quadratic expression into linear expressions
(3) set each linear factor equal to zero and solve
(4) check your solution[s]

A note about factoring quadratics: There are many methods of factoring quadratics, so if you recall a favorite, stick with it. One approach is the "mn" method:

If $x^2 + 2x - 8$ can be factored, it will take the form $(x + m) (x + n)$. To find m and n, set $m + n$ equal to the coefficient of the middle term and mn equal to the last term.

$$m + n = 2$$
$$mn = -8$$

$m = 4$ and $n = -2$ satisfies both equations, therefore $x^2 + 2x - 8 = (x + 4) (x - 2)$. FOIL $(x + 4)$ $(x - 2)$ to confirm that this is correct.

In the example that follows, x is solved for and the solutions are checked:

$$x^2 - 3x = -4x + 12$$
$$x^2 - 3x + 4x - 12 = 0$$
$$x^2 + x - 12 = 0$$
$$(x + 4)(x - 3) = 0$$
$$x + 4 = 0 \text{ and } x - 3 = 0$$
$$x = -4 \text{ and } x = 3$$

$$(4)^2 - 3(-4) = -4(-4) + 12$$
$$16 + 12 = 16 + 12$$
$$28 = 28$$

$$(3)^2 - 3(3) = -4(3) + 12$$
$$9 - 9 = -12 + 12$$
$$0 = 0$$

Sample Question 35: Solve $x^2 + 3x = 6x + 18$ and check your solutions.

(1) put the equation in standard form

$$x^2 + 3x - 6x - 18 = 0$$
$$x^2 - 3x - 18 = 0$$

(2) factor the quadratic equation

$$(x - 6)(x + 3) = 0$$

(3) set each factor equal to zero and solve

$$x - 6 = 0 \text{ and } x + 3 = 0$$
$$x = 6 \text{ and } x = -3$$

(4) check the solutions

$$(6)^2 + 3(6) = 6(6) + 18$$
$$36 + 18 = 36 + 18$$
$$54 = 54$$

$$(-3)^2 + 3(-3) = 6(-3) + 18$$
$$9 - 9 = -18 + 18$$
$$0 = 0$$

PRACTICE SET 22

Solve the following:

1. $x + 3 = 7$

2. $2x - 4 = 14$

3. $2(x + 40) = 100$

4. $5(3x + 14) = 10$

5. $5x + 42 = 3 - 8x$

6. $\dfrac{3}{4}x + 2 = 1$

7. $\dfrac{5}{2}\left(x + \dfrac{8}{5}\right) = \dfrac{3}{2}$

8. $(x + 1)(x - 1) = 0$

9. $\left(m+\dfrac{1}{2}\right)\left(m-\dfrac{1}{2}\right)=0$

10. $12(z + 193)(z - 33) = 0$

11. $(x+2)^2(x-19)=0$

12. $(3x + 2)(x - 2) = 0$

13. $y(y + 1)(y + 2) = 0$

14. $x^2 + 2x + 1 = 0$

15. $2x^2 - 8x + 6 = 0$

16. $m^2 = 9m - 14$

17. $\dfrac{x-1}{2} = 0$

18. $\dfrac{x^2-1}{x-1} = 0$

19. $\dfrac{(2x+3)(x-10)}{x+1} = 0$

20. $\dfrac{n^2+7n+12}{n+4} = 0$

ANSWERS AND EXPLANATIONS—PRACTICE SET 22

1. $x = 4$

$$x + 3 = 7$$
$$x = 7 - 3$$
$$x = 4$$

2. $x = 9$

$$2x - 4 = 14$$
$$2x = 14 + 4$$
$$2x = 18$$
$$x = 9$$

3. $x = 10$

$$2(x + 40) = 100$$
$$x + 40 = \frac{100}{2}$$
$$x + 40 = 50$$
$$x = 50 - 40$$
$$x = 10$$

4. $x = -4$

$$5(3x + 14) = 10$$
$$3x + 14 = \frac{10}{5}$$
$$3x = 2 - 14$$
$$3x = -12$$
$$x = \frac{-12}{3}$$
$$x = -4$$

5. $x = -3$

$$5x + 42 = 3 - 8x$$
$$5x + 8x = 3 - 42$$
$$13x = -39$$
$$x = \frac{-39}{13}$$
$$x = -3$$

6. $x = -\dfrac{4}{3}$

$$\frac{3}{4}x + 2 = 1$$
$$\frac{3}{4}x = 1 - 2$$
$$\frac{3}{4}x = -1$$
$$x = -1\left(\frac{4}{3}\right)$$
$$x = -\frac{4}{3}$$

7. $x = -1$

$$\frac{5}{2}\left(x + \frac{8}{5}\right) = \frac{3}{2}$$
$$x + \frac{8}{5} = \left(\frac{2}{5}\right)\frac{3}{2}$$
$$x = \frac{6}{10} - \frac{8}{5}$$
$$x = \frac{6}{10} - \frac{16}{10}$$
$$x = -\frac{10}{10}$$
$$x = -1$$

8. $x = -1, x = 1$

   $(x+1)(x-1) = 0$

   $x+1 = 0 \Leftrightarrow x-1 = 0 \leftarrow$ set each factor equal to zero

   $x = -1$ or $x = 1 \leftarrow$ solve each mini-equation

   $(-1+1)(-1-1) = 0$ and $(1+1)(1-1) = 0 \leftarrow$ check solutions

9. $m = -\dfrac{1}{2}, m = \dfrac{1}{2}$

   $\left(m+\tfrac{1}{2}\right)\left(m-\tfrac{1}{2}\right) = 0$

   $m+\tfrac{1}{2} = 0 \Leftrightarrow m-\tfrac{1}{2} = 0 \leftarrow$ set each factor equal to zero

   $m = -\tfrac{1}{2}$ or $m = \tfrac{1}{2} \leftarrow$ solve each mini-equation

   $\left(-\tfrac{1}{2}+\tfrac{1}{2}\right)\left(-\tfrac{1}{2}-\tfrac{1}{2}\right) = 0$ and $\left(\tfrac{1}{2}+\tfrac{1}{2}\right)\left(\tfrac{1}{2}-\tfrac{1}{2}\right) = 0 \leftarrow$ check solutions

10. $z = -193, z = 33$

   $12(z+193)(z-33) = 0$

   $z+193 = 0 \Leftrightarrow z-33 = 0 \leftarrow$ set each factor equal to zero

   $z = -193$ or $z = 33 \leftarrow$ solve each mini-equation

   $12(-193+193)(-193-33) = 0$ and $12(33+193)(33-33) = 0 \leftarrow$ check solutions

11. $x = -2, x = 19$

   $(x+2)^2(x-19) = 0$

   $x+2 = 0 \Leftrightarrow x-19 = 0 \leftarrow$ set each factor equal to zero

   $x = -2$ or $x = 19 \leftarrow$ solve each mini-equation

   $(-2+2)^2(-2-19) = 0$ and $(19+2)^2(19-19) = 0 \leftarrow$ check solutions

12. $x = -\dfrac{2}{3}, x = 2$

   $(3x+2)(x-2) = 0$

   $3x+2 = 0 \Leftrightarrow x-2 = 0 \leftarrow$ set each factor equal to zero

   $x = -\tfrac{2}{3}$ or $x = 2 \leftarrow$ solve each mini-equation

   $\left(3\left(-\tfrac{2}{3}\right)+2\right)\left(-\tfrac{2}{3}-2\right) = 0$ and $\left(3(2)+2\right)(2-2) = 0 \leftarrow$ check solutions

13. $y = 0, y = -1, y = -2$

$y(y+1)(y+2) = 0$

$y = 0 \Leftrightarrow y+1 = 0 \Leftrightarrow y+2 = 0 \leftarrow$ set each factor equal to zero

$y = 0$ or $y = -1$ or $y = -2 \leftarrow$ solve each mini-equation

$0(0+1)(0+2) = 0$ and $-1(-1+1)(-1+2) = 0$ and $-2(-2+1)(-2+2) = 0 \leftarrow$ check solutions

14. $x = -1$

$x^2 + 2x + 1 = 0$

$(x+1)(x+1) = 0 \leftarrow$ factor

$x + 1 = 0 \leftarrow$ set repeating factor equal to zero

$x = -1 \leftarrow$ solve mini-equation

$(-1+1)(-1+1) = 0 \leftarrow$ check solution

15. $x = 1, x = 3$

$2x^2 - 8x + 6 = 0$

$2(x^2 - 4x + 3) = 0 \leftarrow$ factor

$2(x-1)(x-3) = 0 \leftarrow$ factor again

$x - 1 = 0 \Leftrightarrow x - 3 = 0 \leftarrow$ set factors equal to zero

$x = 1$ and $x = 3 \leftarrow$ solve each mini-equation

$2(1-1)(1-3) = 0$ and $2(3-1)(3-3) = 0 \leftarrow$ check solutions

16. $m = 2, m = 7$

$m^2 = 9m - 14$

$m^2 - 9m + 14 = 0 \leftarrow$ put equation in standard form

$(m-2)(m-7) = 0 \leftarrow$ factor into linear expressions

$m - 2 = 0 \Leftrightarrow m - 7 = 0 \leftarrow$ set each factor equal to zero

$m = 2$ and $m = 7 \leftarrow$ solve each mini-equation

$(2-2)(2-7) = 0$ and $(7-2)(7-7) = 0 \leftarrow$ check solutions

17. $x = 1$

$\frac{x-1}{2} = 0$

$x - 1 = 0 \leftarrow$ set factor equal to zero

$x = 1 \leftarrow$ solve mini-equation

$\frac{1-1}{2} = 0 \leftarrow$ check solution

18. $x = -1$; x cannot equal 1 because of $x - 1$ in the denominator

$\frac{x^2-1}{x-1} = 0$

$\frac{(x+1)(x-1)}{x-1} = 0 \leftarrow$ factor into linear expressions

$x + 1 = 0 \Leftrightarrow x - 1 = 0 \leftarrow$ set each factor in the numerator equal to zero

$x = -1$ and $x = 1 \leftarrow$ solve each mini - equation

$\frac{(-1+1)(-1-1)}{-1-1} = 0$ but $\frac{(1+1)(1-1)}{1-1} \neq 0 \leftarrow$ check solutions (division by zero is not allowed)

19. $x = -\dfrac{3}{2}, x = 10$

$\frac{(2x+3)(x-10)}{x+1} = 0$

$2x + 3 = 0 \Leftrightarrow x - 10 = 0 \leftarrow$ set each factor in the numerator equal to zero

$x = -\frac{3}{2}$ and $x = 10 \leftarrow$ solve each mini - equation

$\frac{\left(2\left(-\frac{3}{2}\right)+3\right)\left(-\frac{3}{2}-10\right)}{-\frac{3}{2}+1} = 0$ and $\frac{(2(10)+3)(10-10)}{10+1} = 0 \leftarrow$ check solutions

20. $n = -3$; n cannot equal -4 because of the denominator

$\frac{n^2+7n+12}{n+4} = 0$

$(n+3)(n+4) = 0 \leftarrow$ factor numerator into linear expressions

$n + 3 = 0 \Leftrightarrow n + 4 = 0 \leftarrow$ set each factor equal to zero

$n = -3$ and $n = -4 \leftarrow$ solve each mini - equation

$\frac{(-3+3)(-3+4)}{-3+4} = 0$ but $\frac{(-4+3)(-4+4)}{-4+4} \neq 0 \leftarrow$ check solutions (division by zero is not allowed)

Literal Equations

Literal equations are those that contain more than one variable like D = RT. Literal equations are usually solved in terms of one of the variables (like solve for *x* in terms of *y*). Solve literal equations just as you do equations in which there is only one variable; that is, first get the term or terms containing the variable you are solving for on one side of the equation, and then get the variable entirely alone.

Here *x* is solved for in terms of *y*:

$$3x + 2y = \frac{1}{2}y + 5x$$

$$3x - 5x = \frac{y}{2} - 2y$$

$$-2x = -\frac{3y}{2}$$

$$\frac{(-2x)}{-2} = \frac{\left(-\frac{3y}{2}\right)}{-2}$$

$$x = -\frac{3y}{2} \times -\frac{1}{2}$$

$$x = \frac{3}{4}y$$

In the same equation *y* is solved for in terms of *x*:

$$3x + 2y = \frac{1}{2}y + 5x$$

$$2y - \frac{y}{2} = 5x - 3x$$

$$\frac{4y}{2} - \frac{y}{2} = 2x$$

$$\frac{3y}{2} = 2x$$

$$\left(\frac{2}{3}\right)\frac{3y}{2} = \left(\frac{2}{3}\right)2x$$

$$\frac{6y}{6} = \frac{4x}{3}$$

$$y = \frac{4}{3}x$$

PRACTICE SET 23

Solve for the indicated variable:

1. $PV = nrT$ for P

2. $PV = nrT$ for r

3. $a^2 + b^2 = c^2$ for $c, c \geq 0$

4. $a^2 + b^2 = c^2$ for $a, a \geq 0$

5. $r = w(a - b)$ for a

6. $\dfrac{x+1}{y} = y + 1$ for x

7. $\dfrac{ab+c}{bc} = \dfrac{1}{bc}$ for $a, bc \neq 0$

8. $\dfrac{s+q}{r} = q(r+s)$ for s

9. $\dfrac{c+d}{a+b} = a$ for b

10. $d^2 - m^2 = 0$ for d

ANSWERS AND EXPLANATIONS—PRACTICE SET 23

1. $P = \dfrac{nrT}{V}$

   $PV = nrt$

   $P = \dfrac{nrT}{V} \leftarrow$ divide both sides by V

2. $r = \dfrac{PV}{nT}$

   $PV = nrT$

   $\dfrac{PV}{nT} = r \leftarrow$ divide both sides by nT

3. $c = \pm\sqrt{a^2 + b^2}$

   $a^2 + b^2 = c^2$

   $\sqrt{c^2} = \pm\sqrt{a^2 + b^2} \leftarrow$ take the square root of both sides

   $c = \pm\sqrt{a^2 + b^2} \leftarrow$ we are given $c \geq 0$

4. $a = \pm\sqrt{c^2 - b^2}$

   $a^2 + b^2 = c^2$

   $a^2 = c^2 - b^2$

   $\sqrt{a^2} = \pm\sqrt{c^2 - b^2} \leftarrow$ take the square root of both sides

   $a = \pm\sqrt{c^2 - b^2} \leftarrow$ we are given $a \geq 0$

5. $a = \dfrac{r}{w} + b$

   $r = w(a - b)$

   $\dfrac{r}{w} = a - b \leftarrow$ divide both sides by w

   $\dfrac{r}{w} + b = a \leftarrow$ add b to both sides

6. $x = y^2 + y - 1$

$$\frac{x+1}{y} = y + 1$$

$x + 1 = y(y+1)$ ← multiply both sides by y

$x = y(y+1) - 1$ ← subtract 1 from both sides

$x = y^2 + y - 1$ ← simplify

7. $a = \dfrac{1-c}{b}, b \neq 0$

$$\frac{ab+c}{bc} = \frac{1}{bc}$$

$ab + c = \dfrac{bc}{bc}$ ← multiply both sides by bc

$ab = 1 - c$ ← subtract c from both sides

$a = \dfrac{1-c}{b}$ ← divide both sides by b

8. $s = \dfrac{r^2 q - q}{1 - rq}$

$$\frac{s+q}{r} = q(r+s)$$

$s + q = rq(r+s)$ ← multiply both sides by r

$s + q = r^2 q + rqs$ ← distribute rq

$s = r^2 q + rqs - q$ ← subtract q from both sides

$s - rqs = r^2 q - q$ ← subtract rqs from both sides

$s(1-rq) = r^2 q - q$ ← factor out the s

$s = \dfrac{r^2 q - q}{1 - rq}$ ← divide both sides by $1 - rq$

9. $b = \dfrac{c+d-a^2}{a}$

     $\dfrac{c+d}{a+b} = a$

     $c+d = a(a+b)$ ← multiply both sides by $(a+b)$

     $c+d = a^2 + ab$ ← distribute the a

     $c+d-a^2 = ab$ ← subtract a^2 from both sides

     $\dfrac{c+d-a^2}{a} = b$ ← divide both sides by a

10. $d = m, d = -m$

     $d^2 - m^2 = 0$

     $(d-m)(d+m) = 0$ ← difference of two squares

     $d-m = 0 \Leftrightarrow d+m = 0$ ← set each factor equal to 0

     $d = m$ and $d = -m$ ← solve each mini-equation

     $(m-m)(m+m) = 0$ and $(-m-m)(-m+m) = 0$ ← check your solutions

Simultaneous Equations

If you're given two equations that contain two variables, you can use them interactively to solve for the variables. Solving *simultaneous* equations can be done through either substitution or addition.

To solve simultaneous equations by substitution:

(1) solve for one of the variables in terms of the other variable
(2) create a one variable equation by substituting in the value derived and solve
(3) solve for the numerical value of the second variable
(4) check the solutions in both equations

To solve simultaneous equations by addition:

(1) manipulate the equations so that the coefficients of one of the variables are of the same absolute value but of opposite signs
(2) add the equations so that one of the variables cancels out
(3) solve for the numerical value of the second variable
(4) check the solutions in both equations

Sample Question 36: Solve $x + y = 6$ and $3x - y = 10$ simultaneously by substitution

(1) solve for one of the variables in terms of the other variable

$$x + y = 6$$
$$x = 6 - y$$

(2) create a one variable equation by substituting in the value derived and solve

$$3x - y = 10$$
$$3(6 - y) - y = 10$$
$$18 - 3y - y = 10$$
$$-4y = 10 - 18$$
$$y = \frac{-8}{-4}$$
$$y = 2$$

(3) solve for the numerical value of the second variable

$$x + (2) = 6$$
$$x = 6 - 2$$
$$x = 4$$

(4) check the solutions in both equations

$$x + y = 6$$
$$(4) + (2) = 6$$

and

$$3x - y = 10$$
$$3(4) - (2) = 10$$
$$12 - 2 = 10$$

Sample Question 37: Solve $x + y = 6$ and $3x - y = 10$ simultaneously by addition

(1) add the equations so that one of the variables cancels out

$$\begin{aligned} x + \ y &= 6 \\ \underline{3x - \ y} &= \underline{10} \\ 4x - 0y &= 16 \quad \text{(add the two expressions)} \\ 4x &= 16 \\ x &= 4 \end{aligned}$$

(2) solve for the numerical value of the second variable

$$\begin{aligned} 3(4) - y &= 10 \\ 12 - y &= 10 \\ -y &= 10 - 12 \\ -y &= -2 \\ y &= 2 \end{aligned}$$

(3) check the solutions in both equations

$$\begin{aligned} x + y &= 6 \\ (4) + (2) &= 6 \end{aligned}$$

and

$$\begin{aligned} 2x - y &= 10 \\ 3(4) - (2) &= 10 \\ 12 - 2 &= 10 \end{aligned}$$

PRACTICE SET 24

Solve by addition or substitution:

1. $x + y = 2$
   $x - y = 0$

2. $2x + 3y = 8$
   $2x + 5y = 16$

3. $a + b = 2$
   $a - b = -1$

4. $m - 5n = 1$
   $2m + 5n = 47$

5. $x + 4 = 6$
   $2x - 3y = 37$

158

1. $x = 1$
    $y = 1$

$$\begin{bmatrix} x+y=2 \\ x-y=0 \end{bmatrix}$$

Solve for one variable in terms of the other:

$x+y=2$
$\quad x=2-y$

Create a one variable equation and solve:

$\quad\quad x-y=0$
$(2-y)-y=0$
$\quad\quad 2-2y=0$
$\quad\quad\quad -2y=-2$
$\quad\quad\quad\quad y=1$

Solve for the numerical value of the second variable:

$\quad x+y=2$
$x+(1)=2$
$\quad\quad x=1$

Check the solutions in both equations:

$x+y=2$
$1+1=2$
$x-y=0$
$1-1=0$

2. $x = -2$
    $y = 4$

$$\begin{bmatrix} 2x+3y=8 \\ 2x+5y=16 \end{bmatrix}$$

Add the equations so that one of the variables cancels out:

$$2x + 5y = 16$$
$$\underline{+-2x - 3y = -8} \leftarrow \text{multiply each term by} -1$$
$$0 + 2y = 8$$
$$y = 4$$

Solve for the numerical value of the second variable:

$$2x + 3y = 8$$
$$2x + 3(4) = 8$$
$$2x = 8 - 12$$
$$2x = -4$$
$$x = -2$$

Check the solutions in both equations:

$$2x + 3y = 8$$
$$2(-2) + 3(4) = 8$$
$$-4 + 12 = 8$$
$$2x + 5y = 16$$
$$2(-2) + 5(4) = 16$$
$$-4 + 20 = 16$$

3. $a = \dfrac{1}{2}$

$b = \dfrac{3}{2}$

$$\begin{bmatrix} a + b = 2 \\ a - b = -1 \end{bmatrix}$$

Solve for one variable in terms of the other:

$$a + b = 2$$
$$a = 2 - b$$

Create a one variable equation and solve:

$$a - b = -1$$
$$(2 - b) - b = -1$$
$$2 - 2b = -1$$
$$-2b = -3$$
$$b = \frac{3}{2}$$

Solve for the numerical value of the second variable:

$$a - b = -1$$
$$a - \left(\frac{3}{2}\right) = -1$$
$$a = -1 + \frac{3}{2}$$
$$a = -\frac{2}{2} + \frac{3}{2}$$
$$a = \frac{1}{2}$$

Check the solutions in both equations:

$$a + b = 2$$
$$\left(\frac{1}{2}\right) + \left(\frac{3}{2}\right) = 2$$
$$a - b = -1$$
$$\left(\frac{1}{2}\right) - \left(\frac{3}{2}\right) = -1$$
$$-\frac{2}{2} = -1$$

4. $m = 16$

$n = 3$

$$\begin{bmatrix} m - 5n = 1 \\ 2m + 5n = 47 \end{bmatrix}$$

Add the equations so that one of the variables cancels out:

$m - 5n = 1$

$\underline{+2m + 5n = 47}$

$3m + 0 = 48$

$3m = 48$

$m = 16$

Solve for the numerical value of the second variable:

$2m + 5n = 47$

$2(16) + 5n = 47$

$5n = 47 - 32$

$5n = 15$

$n = 3$

Check the solutions in both equations:

$m - 5n = 1$

$(16) - 5(3) = 1$

$16 - 15 = 1$

$2m + 5n = 47$

$2(16) + 5(3) = 47$

$32 + 15 = 47$

5. $x = 2$
    $y = -11$

$$\begin{bmatrix} x + 4 = 6 \\ 2x - 3y = 37 \end{bmatrix}$$

Solve for the numeric value of x using the first equation:

$x + 4 = 6$
$\quad x = 6 - 4$
$\quad x = 2$

Solve for the numerical value of y:

$2x - 3y = 37$
$2(2) - 3y = 37$
$\quad 4 - 3y = 37$
$\quad\quad -3y = 37 - 4$
$\quad\quad -3y = 33$
$\quad\quad\quad y = 11$

Check the solutions in both equations:

$x + 4 = 6$
$\quad 2 = 6 - 4$
$2x - 3y = 37$
$2(2) + 3(11) = 37$
$\quad 4 + 33 = 37$

Inequalities

Linear Inequalities

Expressions joined by <, ≤, >, or ≥ form *inequalities*. Here's a chart for those of you who can't remember what these signs mean:

< means less than ($x < 1$ means x is less than 1)

> means greater than ($x > 1$ means x is greater than 1)

≤ means less than or equal to ($x ≤ 1$ means x is less than or equal to 1)

≥ means greater than or equal to ($x ≥ 1$ means x is greater than or equal to 1)

Inequalities are solved just like equations except that you solve them for a *range* of values and if you multiply or divide both sides of an inequality by a *negative* number, you must *reverse* the direction of the inequality.

If you were told that $-x < 3$, you'd need to divide both sides by -1 to isolate the x, and you'd need to *reverse* the sign. Let's see how it looks:

$$-x < 3$$
$$\frac{-x}{-1} > \frac{3}{-1}$$
$$x > -3$$

The value of x, then, is inclusive of all numbers greater than -3. Here's how that's represented on a number line:

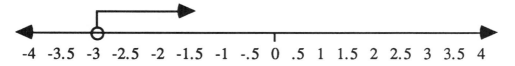

If you were told that $-x < 3$ and $x + 3 ≤ 4$ you could figure out the range of values for x that *satisfy* both inequalities:

$$x + 3 ≤ 4$$
$$x ≤ 4 - 3$$
$$x ≤ 1$$

The value of x, then, is inclusive of all numbers greater than -3, but less than or equal to 1. This can be written $-3 < x ≤ 1$ and would be represented on the number line as follows:

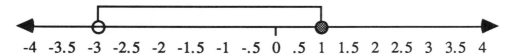

164

Here are a few examples with useful notes:

$$x + 3x - 7 \geq 3$$
$$4x \geq 3 + 7$$
$$4x \geq 10$$
$$\frac{4x}{4} \geq \frac{10}{4}$$
$$x \geq \frac{10}{4}$$
$$x \geq \frac{5}{2}$$

All numbers greater than or equal to $\frac{5}{2}$ satisfy the inequality.

$$3 - \frac{1}{2}x \geq 6$$
$$-\frac{1}{2}x \geq 6 - 3$$
$$(-2)\left(-\frac{1}{2}x\right) \leq (-2)(3)$$
$$x \leq -6$$

Multiplication by -2 requires a reversal of the inequality. All numbers less than or equal to -6 satisfy the inequality.

$$16^{\frac{1}{2}}x + 4x \geq 8$$
$$\sqrt[2]{16}x + 4x \geq 8$$
$$4x + 4x \geq 8$$
$$8x \geq 8$$
$$\frac{8x}{8} \geq \frac{8}{8}$$
$$x \geq 1$$

Recall that fractional exponents denote roots. Numbers equal to or greater than 1 satisfy the inequality.

Quadratic Inequalities

Inequalities containing squared variables are solved much like equations containing squared variables. The expression is set "unequal" to zero, factored and then solved. There are always *two* cases to consider because the variables themselves can be positive or negative. Here are a few examples with useful notes:

$$x^2 > 9$$
$$x^2 - 9 > 0$$
$$(x - 3)(x + 3) > 0$$
$$x - 3 > 0 \text{ and } x + 3 > 0$$
$$\text{or}$$
$$x - 3 < 0 \text{ and } x + 3 < 0$$
$$\text{so}$$
$$x > 3$$
$$\text{or}$$
$$x < -3$$

Here we changed the inequality into the difference of two squares set "unequal" to zero by subtracting 9 from both sides. Since the product of the two factors must be positive, either both factors must be positive, or both must be negative (hence the "and" statements) If they're both positive x must be greater than 3 (greater than -3 would satisfy the $x + 3$ factor but we must satisfy both factors). If they're both negative x must be less than -3 (less than 3 would satisfy the $x - 3$ factor but we must satisfy both factors). Numbers greater than 3, or less than -3, then, satisfy the inequality.

$$2x^2 - 4x - 2 < 4$$
$$2x^2 - 4x - 6 < 0$$
$$2(x^2 - 2x - 3) < 0$$
$$2(x - 3)(x + 1) < 0$$
$$x - 3 < 0 \text{ and } x + 1 > 0$$
$$x < 3 \text{ and } x > -1$$
$$-1 < x < 3$$

Notice that once 4 was subtracted from both sides a common monomial was factored out, and then the trinomial was factored into two binomials. Because the expression must be less than zero, it must multiply to a negative product. Three factors result in a negative product only if either all three factors are negative, or if one of the three is negative. Since the monomial factor (2) is positive, one of the binomials must be negative and the other positive. Because in the first 3 is *subtracted* from x, and in the second 1 is *added* to x, the first must be negative and the second positive. Hence $x - 3 < 0$ and $x + 1 > 0$ and the solution set $-1 < x < 3$. All numbers between -1 and 3 satisfy the inequality.

$$x^2 + 3 - \left(6 + 2^{-1}\right) < 1 - \frac{1}{2}$$

$$x^2 + 3 - \left(6 + \frac{1}{2}\right) < \frac{1}{2}$$

$$x^2 + 3 - \left(6\frac{1}{2}\right) < \frac{1}{2}$$

$$x^2 + 3 - 6\frac{1}{2} < \frac{1}{2}$$

$$x^2 + -3\frac{1}{2} < \frac{1}{2}$$

$$x^2 + -\frac{7}{2} < \frac{1}{2}$$

$$x^2 < \frac{1}{2} + \frac{7}{2}$$

$$x^2 < \frac{8}{2}$$

$$x^2 < 4$$

$$x < 2 \text{ and } x > -2$$

$$-2 < x < 2$$

Since x^2 is less than 4, x can neither be less than -2 nor greater than 2. If x were less than -2, say -3, then x^2 would be greater than 4 instead of less than 4. Similarly, if x were greater than 2, say 4, then x^2 would be greater than 4 instead of less than 4. All numbers between -2 and 2 satisfy the inequality.

Odds and Ends

Here are a few more things about inequalities worth thinking about:

1. If $x < y$ and $y < z$ then $x < z$.

    $7 < 9$ and $9 < 11$ so $7 < 11$

2. If $a < b$ and $x < y$ then $a + x < b + y$

   $3 < 4$ and $7 < 8$ so $3 + 7 < 4 + 8$

3. If $x < y$, and if x and y are of the same sign, then $\frac{1}{x} > \frac{1}{y}$

   $8 < 9$ so $\frac{1}{8} > \frac{1}{9}$

   and

   $-8 > -9$ so $-\frac{1}{8} < -\frac{1}{9}$

Recognizing these relationships will save you time!

Sample Question 38: Find the range of values that satisfy the inequalities: $-2x < 4$ and $x^2 - 3 < 46$

(1) solve the first inequality by isolating x

$$-2x < 4$$
$$\frac{-2x}{2} < \frac{4}{2}$$
$$-x < 2$$
$$(-1)(-x) > (-1)(2)$$
$$x > -2$$

(2) solve the second inequality by isolating x

$$x^2 - 3 < 46$$
$$x^2 < 46 + 3$$
$$x^2 < 49$$
$$x < 7 \text{ and } x > -7$$
$$-7 < x < 7$$

(3) determine which values satisfy both inequalities

$x > -2$ so $-2 < x < 7$ satisfies both inequalities

PRACTICE SET 25

Simplify the following inequalities:

1. $-x < 3$

2. $-y > 4$

3. $2x > 7$

4. $2x + 4 > 18$

5. $x - 6 < 2x - 7$

6. $x^2 - 9 < 0$

7. $x^2 > 16$

8. $x^2 < 25$

9. $3m^2 + 2 < -10 - 15m$

10. $x^2 + 9 < 0$

11. If $q > r$ and $r > s$ and $s > t$, then what is the relationship between

    a. q and t

    b. t and r

    c. $q + s$ and $r + t$

    d. $q - t$ and $r - s$

12. If x and y are the same sign and $x > y$, what is the relationship between the following?

    a. $\dfrac{1}{x}$ and $\dfrac{1}{y}$

    b. $-\dfrac{1}{x}$ and $-\dfrac{1}{y}$

    c. $-\dfrac{1}{x}$ and $\dfrac{1}{y}$

170

ANSWERS AND EXPLANATIONS—PRACTICE SET 25

1. $x > -3$

   $-x < 3$

   $x > -3 \leftarrow$ divide both sides by -1 and reverse the sign

2. $y < -4$

   $-y > 4$

   $y < -4 \leftarrow$ divide both sides by -1 and reverse the sign

3. $x > \dfrac{7}{2}$

   $2x > 7$

   $x > \dfrac{7}{2} \leftarrow$ divide both sides by 2

4. $x > 7$

   $2x + 4 > 18$

   $2x > 14 \leftarrow$ subtract 4 from both sides

   $x > 7 \leftarrow$ divide both sides by 2

5. $x > 1$

   $x - 6 < 2x - 7$

   $-x - 6 < -7 \leftarrow$ subtract $2x$ from both sides

   $-x < -1 \leftarrow$ add 6 to both sides

   $x > 1 \leftarrow$ divide both sides by -1 and reverse the sign

6. $-3 < x < 3$

   $x^2 - 9 < 0$

   $(x + 3)(x - 3) < 0 \leftarrow$ factor

   $x + 3 > 0 \Leftrightarrow x - 3 < 0 \leftarrow$ one factor must be positive and one factor must be negative

   $-3 < x < 3$

7. $x > 4$ or $x < -4$

$x^2 > 16$

$x^2 - 16 > 0 \leftarrow$ subtract 16 from both sides

$(x+4)(x-4) > 0 \leftarrow$ factor

$x + 4 > 0 \Leftrightarrow x - 4 > 0 \leftarrow$ the positive / positive case

$x > 4 \leftarrow$ satisfies the positive / positive case

$x + 4 < 0 \Leftrightarrow x - 4 < 0 \leftarrow$ the negative / negative case

$x < -4 \leftarrow$ satisfies the negative / negative case

8. $-5 < x < 5$

$x^2 < 25$

$x^2 - 25 < 0 \leftarrow$ subtract 25 from both sides

$(x+5)(x-5) < 0 \leftarrow$ factor

$x + 5 > 0 \Leftrightarrow x - 5 < 0 \leftarrow$ one factor must be positive and one factor must be negative

$-5 < x < 5$

9. $-4 < m < -1$

$3m^2 + 2 < -10 - 15m$

$3m^2 + 15m + 12 < 0 \leftarrow$ add $10 + 15m$ to both sides

$3(m^2 + 5m + 4) < 0 \leftarrow$ factor

$3(m+4)(m+1) < 0 \leftarrow$ factor again

$m + 4 > 0 \Leftrightarrow m + 1 < 0 \leftarrow$ one factor must be positive and one factor must be negative

$-4 < m < -1$

10. no solution: $x^2 + 9$ is always greater than 0.

11. a. $q > t$

$q > r > s > t$

b. $t < r$

$t < s < r < q$

c. $q + s > r + t$

$q > r$ and $s > t$ so $q + s > r + t$

d. $q - t > r - s$

$q > r$ and $t < s$ so $q - t > r - s$ ← we are starting with more(q), and taking away less(t)

12. a. $\dfrac{1}{x} < \dfrac{1}{y}$

Since x and y are of the same sign and $x > y$ $\dfrac{1}{x} < \dfrac{1}{y}$

b. $-\dfrac{1}{x} > -\dfrac{1}{y}$

Since x and y are of the same sign and $x > y$ $-\dfrac{1}{x} > -\dfrac{1}{y}$

c. cannot be determined, depends on whether x and y are positive or negative

Function Problems

Functions in Disguise

Instead of $f(x, y)$, you may see unusual symbols between the variables like $x \dagger y$ or $x \, \Omega \, y$ or $x \bullet y$. Treat problems involving such symbols exactly like you treat function problems. These examples simply convey the information $f(x, y)$. Most function problems which you will encounter involve two variables. To solve function problems plug the given numerical values into the places their respective variables occur in the original formula. Here are two function problems:

If $f(x) = x^2 + 2x + 1$, what is the value of $f(2)$?

$f(2) = 2^2 + 2(2) + 1$

$f(2) = 4 + 4 + 1$

$f(2) = 9$

If $f(x,y) = \dfrac{3(x + y) + 5\sqrt{x}}{2(x - y) + 4\sqrt{y}}$, what is the value of $f(4,1)$?

$f(4,1) = \dfrac{3(4 + 1) + 5\sqrt{4}}{2(4 - 1) + 4\sqrt{1}}$

$f(4,1) = \dfrac{3(5) + 5\sqrt{4}}{2(3) + 4\sqrt{1}}$

$f(4,1) = \dfrac{3(5) + 5(2)}{2(3) + 4(1)}$

$f(4,1) = \dfrac{15 + 10}{6 + 4}$

$f(4,1) = \dfrac{25}{10}$

$f(4,1) = 2\dfrac{1}{2}$

Here are two function problems:

If $x \dagger y = 4 - \dfrac{x}{y}$, what is the value of $6 \dagger \dfrac{1}{2}$?

$x \dagger y = 4 - \dfrac{6}{\frac{1}{2}}$

$x \dagger y = 4 - \dfrac{6}{1} \div \dfrac{1}{2}$

$x \dagger y = 4 - \dfrac{6}{1} \times \dfrac{2}{1}$

$x \dagger y = 4 - 12$

$x \dagger y = -8$

If $x \oplus y \oplus z = \dfrac{3x + 2y\sqrt{y} + (4 + 5x)}{z + 1}$, what is the value of $4 \oplus 9 \oplus 14$?

$4 \oplus 9 \oplus 14 = \dfrac{3(4) + 2(9)\sqrt{9} + (4 + 5(4))}{14 + 1}$

$4 \oplus 9 \oplus 14 = \dfrac{12 + 2(9)(3) + (4 + 20)}{15}$

$4 \oplus 9 \oplus 14 = \dfrac{12 + 2(27) + (24)}{15}$

$4 \oplus 9 \oplus 14 = \dfrac{12 + 54 + 24}{15}$

$4 \oplus 9 \oplus 14 = \dfrac{90}{15}$

$4 \oplus 9 \oplus 14 = 6$

PRACTICE SET 26

1. $f(x) = 2x^2 + x - 1$; find $f(-1)$

2. $f(x,y) = \dfrac{x^2 - y^2}{x - y}$; find $f(2,3)$

3. $r \oplus s = \dfrac{r}{s} + \dfrac{s}{r}$; find $\dfrac{1}{2} \oplus -\dfrac{1}{2}$

4. $x \, \Omega \, y = \dfrac{xy - y}{xy + y}$; find $5 \, \Omega \, 10$

5. $a \# b = a^2 + 2ab + b^2$; find $x \# 2$

6. $t \parallel v = \dfrac{t-v}{t+v}$; find $3a \parallel 2a$

7. $x \ominus y = x^2 - y^2$; find $0.1 \ominus 0.1$

176

ANSWERS AND EXPLANATIONS—PRACTICE SET 26

1. 0

$$f(x) = 2x^2 + x - 1$$
$$f(-1) = 2(-1)^2 + (-1) - 1$$
$$= 2(1) - 1 - 1$$
$$= 0$$

2. 5

$$f(x, y) = \frac{x^2 - y^2}{x - y}$$
$$f(2, 3) = \frac{(2)^2 - (3)^2}{(2) - (3)}$$
$$= \frac{4 - 9}{-1}$$
$$= \frac{-5}{-1}$$
$$= 5$$

3. -2

$$r \oplus s = \frac{r}{s} + \frac{s}{r}$$
$$\frac{1}{2} \oplus -\frac{1}{2} = \frac{\frac{1}{2}}{-\frac{1}{2}} + \frac{-\frac{1}{2}}{\frac{1}{2}}$$
$$= \frac{-\frac{1}{2} - \frac{1}{2}}{\frac{1}{2}}$$
$$= \frac{-\frac{2}{2}}{\frac{1}{2}}$$
$$= -1 \times 2$$
$$= -2$$

4. $\dfrac{2}{3}$

$$x \Omega y = \frac{xy - y}{xy + y}$$

$$5 \Omega 10 = \frac{(5)(10) - (10)}{(5)(10) + (10)}$$

$$= \frac{50 - 10}{50 + 10}$$

$$= \frac{40}{60}$$

$$= \frac{2}{3}$$

5. $x^2 + 4x + 4$

$$a \# b = a^2 + 2ab + b^2$$

$$x \# 2 = (x)^2 + 2(x)(2) + (2)^2$$

$$= x^2 + 4x + 4$$

6. $\dfrac{1}{5}$

$$t \parallel v = \frac{t - v}{t + v}$$

$$3a \parallel 2a = \frac{3a - 2a}{3a + 2a}$$

$$= \frac{a}{5a}$$

$$= \frac{1}{5}$$

7. 0

$$x \Theta y = x^2 - y^2$$

$$0.1 \Theta 0.1 = (0.1)^2 - (0.1)^2$$

$$= 0$$

Word Problems

Introduction

Familiarize yourself with each of the following types of word problems: basic arithmetic/algebra, percent/ratio/proportion, motion, work, set and sequence. You've encountered some of these kinds of word problems in prior practice sets, but you've not had an overall review, which is what this section is intended to accomplish. The most important part of solving a word problem is understanding exactly what's being asked for and setting the problem up correctly. Solving word problems once they're set up is usually a breeze. The key to setting up word problems is the proper translation of words and phrases into algebraic symbols.

Sentence in English	Sentence in Algebra
Alpha is half Beta's age.	$A = \frac{1}{2}B$
35% of the apples are rotten.	$.35N$ (where N = number of apples)
Dancer weighs 20 pounds more than Hunter.	$D = H + 20$
Austin makes 500 dollars less than George.	$A = G - \$500$
Sandra makes twice as much as Alec.	$S = 2(A)$
Six out of every ten voted for the proposition.	$\frac{6}{10}$
A certain number is 3 less than 25% of z.	$x = .25z - 3$

Here is a chart to summarize the translations exemplified above:

equals, is	=
sum, more than	+
difference, less than	−
times, of, product	×
quotient, per, ratio	÷

To solve word problems:

(1) determine what's being asked for
(2) determine all of the givens
(3) sketch the relationships presented
(4) decide which formulas are relevant
(5) set up the algebraic equation[s]
(6) solve and make sure your solution makes sense

(Note: Not all of these steps are necessary on all word problems.)

Basic Word Problems

Basic word problems require you to add, subtract, multiply and divide. Here are a few examples of basic word problems, and the equations that can be used to solve them. (Keep in mind that most word problems can be solved more than one way.)

Sample Question 39: Lou's books cost four times what Sara's books cost. Sara's books cost four times what Patrick's books cost. Patrick's books cost four dollars more than Jay's books, which cost $18.00. How much did Lou's books cost?

(1) determine what's being asked for

   the price of Lou's books

(2) determine all of the givens

   L's books cost 4 times what Sara's cost
   Sara's books cost 4 times what Patrick's cost
   Patrick's books cost 4 more dollars than Jay's books
   Jay's books cost $18

(3) set up the equations
   L = 4S
   S = 4P
   P = J + $4

(4) solve and make sure your solution makes sense
   P = $18 + $4 = $22
   S = 4($22) = $88
   L = 4($88) = $352

Sample Question 40: If Jaston is 16 years younger than Peyton and Peyton is 3 years older than Ki, who is 2 years over one quarter of a century old, how old is Miguel, who is 3 years shy of one-half Jaston's age?

(1) determine what's being asked for

Miguel's age

(2) determine all of the givens

Jaston is 16 years younger than Peyton.
Peyton is 3 years older than Ki.
Ki is $25 + 2 = 27$ years old.
Miguel is 3 years shy of half Jaston's age.

(3) set up the equations

$J = P - 16$ (We subtract 16 because Jaston is younger than Peyton.)
$P = K + 3$ (We add 3 because Peyton is older than Ki.)
$K = 27$
$M = \frac{1}{2}J - 3$

(4) solve and make sure your solution makes sense

$P = 27 + 3 = 30$
$J = 30 - 16 = 14$
$M = \frac{1}{2}(14) - 3$
$M = 7 - 3 = 4$

Percent/Ratio/Proportion Word Problems

There are several percent/ratio/proportion word problems in the practice sets in the sections of this book entitled "Percents" and "Ratios." Here are the basic formulas and processes to remember:

1. part = percent × whole

2. % change = $\dfrac{\text{amount of change}}{\text{original amount}} \times 100$

3. profit = selling price − cost

4. $\dfrac{\text{discount}}{\text{markup amount}} = \dfrac{\text{percent off}}{\text{added}} \times$ usual price

5. to distribute a whole across a ratio divide the whole by the number of total parts and multiply the resulting quotient by each part of the ratio

6. to find a missing term of a proportion cross multiply (flip one fraction before cross multiplying if the proportions are inversely related)

Motion Word Problems

The formula for solving most motion word problems is, of course, Distance = Rate × Time. Here is the formula in its three variations:

$$\text{Distance} = \text{Rate} \times \text{Time}$$

$$\text{Rate} = \frac{\text{Distance}}{\text{Time}}$$

$$\text{Time} = \frac{\text{Distance}}{\text{Rate}}$$

Sample Question 41: If Diego ran a 10 mile road race in 92 minutes, and he ran averaged a 6 minute per mile pace for the first 2 miles, what speed did he average, in miles per hour, for the last 8 miles of the race?

(1) determine what's being asked for

Diego's average rate in MPH for the last 8 miles of the race

(2) determine all of the givens

Diego ran 10 miles in 92 minutes
Diego ran the first 2 miles in 12 minutes

(3) sketch the relationships presented

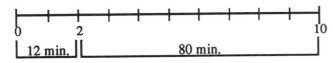

(4) decide which formulas are relevant (including conversions)

$$\text{Rate} = \frac{\text{Distance}}{\text{Time}}$$

60 min. = 1 hour

(5) set up the equations

Distance = 10 miles – 2 miles

Time = 92 minutes – 12 minutes

$$R = \frac{8 \text{ miles}}{80 \text{ minutes}}$$

(6) solve and make sure your solution makes sense

$$\text{Rate} = \frac{\overset{1}{\cancel{8}} \text{ miles}}{\underset{1}{\cancel{80}} \text{ minutes}} \times \frac{\overset{6}{\cancel{60}} \text{ minutes}}{1 \text{ hour}} = \frac{6 \text{ miles}}{1 \text{ hour}}$$

182

Sample Question 42: At noon, Sheila travels due west from point A on a train going 60 miles per hour and Martha travels due east from point A in bus going 30 miles per hour. At what time will the two be exactly 450 miles apart?

(1) determine what's being asked for

the time at which the distance between the 2 women will be 450 miles

(2) determine all the givens

$$Rate_S = 60 \text{ mph}$$
$$Rate_M = 30 \text{ mph}$$
$$Distance_{total} = 450 \text{ miles}$$

(3) sketch the relationships presented

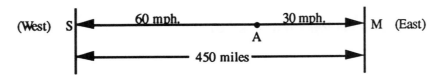

(4) decide which formulas are relevant

$D = R \times T$

$D_{total} = D_S + D_M$

D Total = Distance between Sheila and Martha
Ds = Distance Sheila from point A
Dm = Distance Martha from point A

$D_S = R_S \times T$

$D_M = R_M \times T$

(5) set up the equations

$D_S = 60 \text{mph} \times T$

$D_M = 30 \text{mph} \times T$

(6) solve and make sure your answers make sense

$$D_{total} = 60T + 30T$$
$$D_{total} = 90T$$
$$450 \text{ miles} = 90T$$
$$T = \frac{450 \text{ miles}}{90 \text{ mph}}$$
$$T = 5 \text{ hours}$$

Work Word Problems

Work problems usually require you to set up a ratio. Recall that ratios involving work are usually inversely related: the more workers you have, the less time it takes to get the job done.

Two examples follow, in the first, assume the boys work at the same rate, and in the second, assume that Hans and Donna are working "together, though independently" at their respective rates.

Example 1

If a boy can paint a fence in 4 hours, how long would it take 3 boys to paint the fence?

More boys will be painting, so the painting will take *less* time. The terms of the proportion vary indirectly:

$$\frac{1 \text{ boy}}{3 \text{ boys}} = \frac{x \text{ hours}}{4 \text{ hours}} \text{ (the second ratio is inverted)}$$
$$4 = 3x \text{ (cross multiply)}$$
$$x = \frac{4}{3}$$
$$x = 1\frac{1}{3} \text{ hours or 1 hour and 20 minutes}$$

Example 2

If Hans can tile the floor in 6 hours, and Donna can tile the floor in 4 hours, how long should it take them to tile the floor if they work together, though independently?

Hans works at the rate of $\frac{1}{6}$ of the job per hour (it takes him 6 hours to tile the floor), while Donna works at the rate of $\frac{1}{4}$ of the job per hour (it takes her 4 hours to tile the floor). Together, then, they average a rate of $\frac{1}{6} + \frac{1}{4} = \frac{2}{12} + \frac{3}{12} = \frac{5}{12}$ of the job per hour. To figure out how long it will take them to do the job working at that rate, simply flip the fraction. (It takes them x hours working at the rate of $\frac{5}{12}$ of the job per hour to complete the job so $\frac{5}{12}x = 1$ job and $x = \frac{12}{5}$ hours or 2 and $\frac{2}{5}$ hours or 2 hours and 24 minutes.

Sample Question 43: If 9 artists can paint a mural in 15 days, how long would it take 6 artists?

(1) determine what's being asked for

time (in days) it will take 6 artists to paint a mural

(2) determine all the givens

it takes 9 artists 15 days
we have only 6 artists

(3) set up the equation

$$\frac{9 \text{ artists}}{6 \text{ artists}} = \frac{x \text{ days}}{15 \text{ days}} \text{ (the second ratio is inverted)}$$

(4) solve and make sure your answer makes sense

$$\frac{9 \text{ artists}}{6 \text{ artists}} = \frac{x \text{ days}}{15 \text{ days}}$$
$$9(15) = 6x$$
$$135 = 6x$$
$$x = \frac{135}{6}$$
$$x = 22\frac{1}{2} \text{ days}$$

Set Word Problems

Set problems are generally designed to illustrated principles of *overlapping sets*. If you are told that 16 girls signed up for candle making, 12 signed up for woodwork, and 6 signed up for both, you can deduce that $16 - 6 = 10$ signed up for candle making but not woodwork and $12 - 6 = 6$ signed up for woodwork but not candle making. You can also deduce that 10 (candle making only) + 6 (woodwork only) + 6 (both) = 22 girls (not 34) signed up for the activities. These relationships can be displayed graphically:

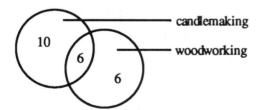

Recognizing overlap in sets helps you to avoid mistakenly accounting for certain elements twice.

Sample Question 44: If 40 of the 100 respondents to the survey said that they had attended Mardi Gras last year, 60 said they had attended New Orleans Jazzfest last year, and 25 said they had attended both, how many said they had attended neither?

(1)   determine what's being asked

   # out of the 100 that attended neither Mardi Gras nor the Jazzfest last year

(2)   determine the givens

   100 survey respondents
   40 Mardi Gras
   60 Jazzfest
   25 both

(3)   sketch the relationships presented

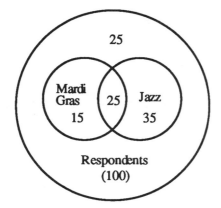

(4)   set up the equations

$$N_{mg\ only} = N_{mg} - N_{both}$$
$$N_{jazz\ only} = N_{jazz} - N_{both}$$
$$N_{neither} = N_{resp} - N_{both} - N_{mg\ only} - N_{jazz\ only}$$

(5)   solve and make sure your answers make sense

$$N_{mg\ only} = 40 - 25 = 15$$
$$N_{jazz\ only} = 60 - 25 = 35$$
$$N_{neither} = 100 - 25 - 15 - 35 = 25$$
$$N_{neither} = 25$$

Another type of set problem tests your ability to consider all possible *combinations*. Suppose, for instance, that Jack Lantern has 3 sets of funny teeth, 6 pairs of unusual eye wear and 9 wigs from which he will choose to dress up for Halloween. If Jack Lantern wants to test every possible combination of the three items, then he would have to test $3 \times 6 \times 9 = 162$ different combinations. If you are faced with a question asking for the number of possible combinations, just remember to *multiply* the different elements.

PRACTICE SET 27

1. Alexa's car cost three times as much as Pete's motorcycle. Pete's motorcycle cost half as much as Jennifer's car. Jennifer's car cost $3,000. How much did Alexa's car cost?

2. Joyce is twice Dora's age. Dora is 5 years older than Karen. Karen just turned 21 years old. How old is Joyce?

3. Jake is 25 years younger than his father. Jake is $\frac{1}{8}$ the age of his mother. His mother is three years older than his father. How old is Jake?

4. Last year Amy's team won 7 more games than Steve's team did. Dan's team won twice as many games as Steve's team did. Steve's team won 5 games. How many more wins did Amy's team have than Dan's team had?

5. Janeen's car gets 18 miles per gallon using a brand of gasoline that costs $1.20 per gallon. How far can she drive her car on $6.00 worth of this brand of gasoline?

6. Sharon drove 90 miles in one and one half hours. After one hour she had driven 55 miles. What was her average speed for the rest of the trip?

7. Roman leaves a rest area and travels due north at 65 miles per hour. Lori leaves the rest area at the same time, traveling 55 miles per hour due south. How many hours after they leave the rest area will they be 300 miles apart?

8. A jet airplane and a propeller airplane pass close to each other going in opposite directions. The jet is flying four times as fast as the propeller airplane. After two hours of flying in opposite directions, the airplanes are 1,500 miles apart. How fast is the propeller airplane flying?

9. If it takes one person 3 hours to plow a field, how long would it take four people to plow the same field?

10. If three of a certain type of pump can empty a tank in 8 hours, then how long would it take four pumps of the same type to empty the same tank?

11. Out of a class of 84 students, 52 students have at least one brother, 50 students have at least one sister, and 25 students have at least one brother and one sister.

    a.   How many students have at least one brother, but no sisters?

    b.   How many students have at least one sister, but no brothers?

    c.   How many students do **not** have any brothers or sisters?

12. In a survey of 290 drivers, 80% admitted they had been ticketed for speeding, 50% admitted they had been ticketed for moving violations other than speeding, and 40% admitted they had been ticketed for speeding and moving violations other than speeding.

    a.   How many drivers surveyed admitted to being ticketed for speeding?

    b.   How many drivers surveyed admitted to being ticketed for a moving violation other than speeding?

c. How many drivers surveyed admitted to being ticketed for speeding but **not** for a moving violation?

d. What percentage of drivers surveyed did **not** admit to receiving any tickets for speeding or other moving violations?

13. A five pound mixture of barley and oats is $\frac{4}{5}$ oats by weight. How much barley (in pounds) must be added to the mixture to make it $\frac{3}{5}$ oats by weight?

14. In a candy store, bubble gum costs 5 cents apiece and jawbreakers cost 4 cents apiece. At these prices a 25 piece mixed bag of bubble gum and jawbreakers goes for $1.15. How many jawbreakers are there in the bag?

15. At a health club, memberships cost 18 dollars a month. Currently, the health club has 100 members. How many more members would the health club need to ensure that total membership receipts exceed $2,550?

16. It takes Justin 5 hours to clean the shop. It takes Philip 3 hours to clean the shop. How long would it take the two, working together but at their independent rates, to clean the shop?

ANSWERS—PRACTICE SET 27

1. $4,500. Let A = the cost of Alexa's car. Let P = the cost of Pete's motorcycle, and let J = the cost of Jennifer's car. Since Alexa's car cost three times as much as Pete's motorcycle, A = 3P. Since Pete's motorcycle cost half as much as Jennifer's car, $P = \frac{1}{2}J$. Since Jennifer's car cost $3,000, J = $3,000. Using the value of J to determine P we get $P = \frac{1}{2}(\$3,000) = \$1,500$. Using the value of P to determine the value of A we get A = 3($1,500) = $4,500. Alexa's car cost $4,500.

2. 52 years old. Let J = Joyce's age. Let D = Dora's age, and let K = Karen's age. Joyce is twice Dora's age, so J = 2D. Dora is 5 years older than Karen, so D = K + 5. Since Karen is 21, Dora must be 26 (21 + 5 = 26), and Joyce must be 52 (2 (26) = 52).

3. 4 years old. Let J = Jake's age. Let F = Jake's father's age and let M = Jake's mother's age. Since Jake is twenty five years younger than his father, J = F – 25. Since Jake is 1/8 the age of his mother, Jake $= \frac{1}{8}M$. Since Jake's mother is three years older than his father, M = F + 3. $J = \frac{1}{8}M$ and M = F + 3, so J = 1/8(F + 3). J also = F – 25. So:

$$F - 25 = \frac{1}{8}(F + 3)$$

$$8(F - 25) = F + 3$$

$$8F - 200 = F + 3$$

$$7F = 203$$

$$F = \frac{203}{7}$$

$$F = 29$$

Since J = F – 25, J = 29 – 25, J = 4.

4. 2. Let A = the number of wins for Amy's team. Let S = the number of wins for Steve's team, and let D = the number of wins for Dan's team. Since Amy's team won 7 more games than Steve's team, A = S + 7. Since Dan's team won twice as many games as Steve's team, D = 2(S). Steve's team won 5 games, so S = 5. We are looking for (A – D) so we must find A and D. A = 12 because 5 + 7 = 12. D = 10 because 2(5) = 10. 12 – 10 = 2, so Amy's team has two more wins than Dan's team.

5. 90. This problem can be solved as a direct proportion. (The *more* gas that is purchased, the *more* miles that can be traveled.)

$$\frac{x}{18 \text{ miles}} = \frac{6 \text{ dollars}}{1.2 \text{ dollars}}$$

$$1.2x = 18(6)$$

$$1.2x = 108$$

$$x = \frac{108}{1.2}$$

$$x = 90$$

Another way to solve the problem is to first determine how many gallons were purchased with six dollars:

$$\frac{6.00}{1.20} = 5 \text{ gallons}$$

And then to determine how many miles 5 gallons of gas will take you given 18 miles per gallon. $(5)(18) = 90$ miles.

6. 70. We are looking for Sharon's "rate" on the second part of the trip. "Distance" and "time" can be figured from what is given:

$$\text{Rate} = \frac{\text{Distance}}{\text{Time}}$$

$D_{(\text{part 2})} = D_{(\text{total})} - D_{(\text{part 1})}$

$D_{(\text{part 2})} = 90 - 55 = 35$ miles

$T_{(\text{part 2})} = T_{(\text{total})} - T_{(\text{part 1})}$

$T_{(\text{part 2})} = 1\frac{1}{2}$ hours $- 1$ hour $= \frac{1}{2}$ hour

$\text{Rate}_{(\text{part 2})} = \dfrac{35 \text{ miles}}{.5 \text{ hours}}$

$\text{Rate}_{(\text{part 2})} = 70$ mph

7. 2.5. The total distance between Roman and Lori is equal to the distance Roman traveled plus the distance Lori traveled.

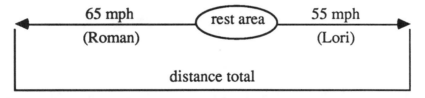

Roman's distance equals his (rate) (time) or 65T. Lori's distance equals her (rate) (time) or 55T. The total distance (300 miles) equals 65T + 55T.

$300 = 65T + 55T$

$300 = 120T$

$T = \dfrac{300}{120}$

$T = 2.5$ (in $2\frac{1}{2}$ hours they'll be 300 miles apart)

8. 150. The jet airplane and the propeller airplane are flying in opposite directions from a given point (the point at which they pass one another). As in problem number 7, we are dealing with total distance (1,500 miles). The total distance is equal to the distance the jet airplane flies plus the distance the propeller airplane flies. The jet flies four times as

fast as the propeller so let the jet rate = 4P, and the propeller rate = P. The time is 2 hours for both airplanes, so D jet = 4P(2) and D propeller = P(2).

$$D_{total} = D_{jet} + D_{propeller}$$

$$1500 = 4P(2) + P(2)$$

$$1500 = 8P + 2P$$

$$1500 = 10P$$

$$P = \frac{1500}{10}$$

$$P = 150$$

The propeller airplane's rate must be 150 mph.

9. 45 minutes. This is a work problem. The ratio here is inverse because the *more* people that plow, the *less* time the plowing takes.

$$\frac{1 \text{ person}}{4 \text{ people}} = \frac{x \text{ hours}}{3 \text{ hours}}$$

$$3 = 4x$$

$$x = \frac{3}{4} \text{ or 45 minutes}$$

10. 6 hours. This is also a work problem. Again, the ratio is inverse because the more pumps there are working, the less amount of time it takes to empty the tank.

$$\frac{3 \text{ pumps}}{4 \text{ pumps}} = \frac{x \text{ hours}}{8 \text{ hours}}$$

$$24 = 4x$$

$$x = 6 \text{ hours}$$

11. a. 27. To find out how many of the 84 students have at least one brother but no sisters, subtract the number of students that have both from the number that have at least one brother:

brother only = brother – both

$$= 52 - 25$$

$$= 27$$

b. 25. To find out how many of the 84 students have at least one sister but no brother, subtract the number of students that have both from the number that have at least one sister:

sister only = sister – both

$$= 50 - 25$$

$$= 25$$

c. 7. To find out how many students do not have any brothers or sisters, total the three sub-sums (those that have only brother(s), those that have only sister(s), those that have both) and subtract the sum from the number of students in the class (84).

$$\text{\# with no siblings} = \text{total} - [(\text{brothers only}) + (\text{sisters only}) + (\text{both})]$$
$$= 84 - [(27) + (25) + (25)]$$
$$= 84 - 77$$
$$= 7$$

12. a. 232. We are looking for the part who admitted to being ticketed for speeding so use the formula: part = %(whole).

part = 80%(290)

part = .8(290)

part = 232

b. 145. We are looking for the part who admitted to being ticketed for a moving violation other than speeding so use the formula: part = %(whole).

part = 50%(290)

part = .5(290)

part = 145

c. 116. We are looking for the part that admitted to being ticketed for speeding but not for a moving violation other than speeding. 80% admitted to being ticketed for speeding and 40% admitted to being ticketed for both, so 80% − 40% = 40% admitted to being ticketed for speeding but not for a moving violation other than speeding. Now use the part = %(whole) formula:

part = 40%(290)

part = .4(290)

part = 116

d. 10%. We are looking for the percentage of drivers that did not admit to receiving any tickets for speeding or other moving violations. Total the three sub-percents (those who only admitted to being ticketed for speeding, those who only admitted to being ticketed for a moving violation other than speeding, and those that admitted to being ticketed for both) and subtract the sum from the number of drivers surveyed (100%).

% that did not admit to receiving tickets = 100% − [% speeding only + % other only + % both]

% speeding only = % speeding − % both
% speeding only = 80% − 40%
% speeding only = 40%

% other moving only = % other moving only − % both
% other moving only = 50% − 40%
% other moving only = 10%

% both = 40% (given)

= 100% − [40% + 10% + 40%]

= 100% − 90%

= 10%

13. $1\frac{2}{3}$. First convert the fractions to percents. The original mixture was $\frac{80\% \text{ oats}}{20\% \text{ barley}}$ and the new mixture will be $\frac{60\% \text{ oats}}{40\% \text{ barley}}$. Let b = the number of pounds of barley to be added. The amount of oats in the new mixture will be the same as the amount of oats in the original mixture (.8)(5), because barley is what will be added. The number of pounds of the new mixture will be (5 + b). Since oats will represent (.6) of the new mixture, you can set up the following part to whole ratio to solve for b:

$$\frac{(.8)(5)}{5+b} = 60\%$$

$$\frac{(.8)(5)}{5+b} = .6$$

$$(.8)(5) = .6(5 + b)$$

$$4 = 3 + .6b$$

$$.6b = 4 - 3$$

$$.6b = 1$$

$$b = \frac{1}{.6}$$

$$b = 1\frac{2}{3} \text{ (lbs. of barley must be added)}$$

14. 10. Let g = the number of pieces of gum in the bag and let j = the number of jawbreakers in the bag. Two equations, solved simultaneously, allow us to determine the number of jawbreakers in the bag.

$$g + j = 25$$
$$.05g + .04j = 1.15$$

Solve for g in terms of j and then use substitution to determine the numerical value of j.

$$g = 25 - j$$
$$.05(25 - j) + .04j = 1.15$$
$$1.25 - .05j + .04j = 1.15$$
$$1.25 - 1.15 = .05j - .04j$$
$$.1 = .01j$$
$$j = \frac{.1}{.01}$$
$$j = 10$$

There are 10 jawbreakers in the 25 piece bag.

15. $41\frac{2}{3}$. Let x = the number of new members needed. Total receipts must be $18(100 + x)$. Since total receipts must exceed 2,550, the following inequality can be used to solve for the values that satisfy x:

$$18(100 + x) > 2,550$$
$$1,800 + 18x > 2,550$$
$$18x > 2,550 - 1,800$$
$$18x > 750$$
$$x > \frac{750}{18}$$
$$x > 41\frac{2}{3}$$

At least 42 new members are needed to bring the membership receipts to a number exceeding $2,550.

16. 1 hour $52\frac{1}{2}$ minutes. Let x = the number of hours it takes Justin and Philip to clean the shop together. Since it takes Justin 5 hours to clean the shop, Justin can do $\frac{1}{5}$ of the job in 1 hour. Since it takes Philip 3 hours to clean the shop, Philip can do $\frac{1}{3}$ of the job in 1 hour. In 1 hour the guys can complete $\frac{1}{x}$ of the job, so

$$\frac{1}{x} = \frac{1}{5} + \frac{1}{3}$$

$$\frac{1}{x} = \frac{3}{15} + \frac{5}{15}$$

$$\frac{1}{x} = \frac{8}{15}$$

$$x = \frac{15}{8} \text{ hours}$$

$$x = 1\frac{7}{8} \text{ hours}$$

$$x = 1 \text{ hour } 52\frac{1}{2} \text{ minutes}$$

PART 3: GEOMETRY

Coordinate Geometry

The Plane

A coordinate plane consists of a number line with a vertical number line cutting through the middle of it. The two number lines (they're actually called *axes*), intersect one another at their respective zeros, and are perpendicular, that is; the angles created by their intersection are 90° each. The axes, and the area around the axes form a four quartered plane. Each quarter is called a *quadrant*. The horizontal axis (our original number line) is called the *x-axis*, and the vertical axis (the newcomer) is called the *y-axis*. Axes and planes are useful for plotting *coordinates*, or ordered pairs of numbers representing the *x* and *y* values of points. The coordinates of the *origin* are (0, 0). The *x* coordinate is written first, and the *y* coordinate is written second. Positive *x* values mean movement to the right from the origin and negative *x* values mean movement to the left (just like on a number line). Positive *y* values mean movement up from the origin, and negative *y* values mean movement down. If you were told to plot the ordered pair (3, -6), you'd count 3 to the right on the *x*-axis, and 6 down from that on the *y*-axis. Your point, then, representing the ordered pair (3, -6) would be over to the right and down twice as much as over from the origin.

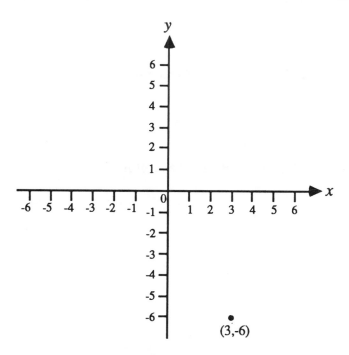

Here are a few things to remember about ordered pairs:

1. If either or both of the coordinates are 0, then the point lies on one or both of the axes.

2. If both coordinates are positive, then the point lies to the right and above the origin.

3. If both coordinates are negative, then the point lies to the left and below the origin.

4. If the x-coordinate is positive and the y-coordinate is negative, then the point lies to the right and below the origin.

5. If the x-coordinate is negative and the y-coordinate is positive, then the point lies to the left and above the origin.

Distance and Midpoint

You may come across questions that require you to determine the *distance* between two points. It's easy to determine the distance between two points on a single number line, but determining the distance between points on a grid requires the following formula:

$$d = \sqrt{(x_2 - x_1)^2 + (y_2 - y_1)^2}$$

The distance between the point plotted above (3, -6) and a second point, say (-5, 2), would thus be determined as follows:

$d = \sqrt{(-5 - 3)^2 + (2 - (-6))^2}$
$d = \sqrt{(-8)^2 + (8)^2}$
$d = \sqrt{64 + 64}$
$d = \sqrt{128}$
$d = \sqrt{64 \times 2}$
$d = 8\sqrt{2}$

To find the *midpoint* between two points, simply add the x coordinates together, and divide by 2, and add the y coordinates together, and divide by 2. Here's the formula:

coordinates of the midpoint between points 1 and 2 $= \dfrac{x_1 + x_2}{2}, \dfrac{y_1 + y_2}{2}$

So the midpoint between the points (3, -6) and (-5, 2) is determined as follows:

$\text{midpoint} = \dfrac{3 + -5}{2}, \dfrac{-6 + 2}{2}$
$\text{midpoint} = \dfrac{-2}{2}, \dfrac{-4}{2}$
$\text{midpoint} = (-1, -2)$

As you can see, the point (-1, -2) is right in the middle of our other two points:

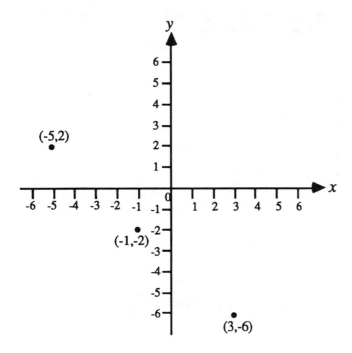

PRACTICE SET 28

1. In the diagram below, each of the four quadrants has been assigned a number. Determine in which quadrant each of the following points lie.

a. (1, 1)
b. (-4, -16)
c. (-2, -3)
d. (6, 8)
e. (-7, 3)
f. (4, -6)
g. (60, -1)
h. (-1, 17)

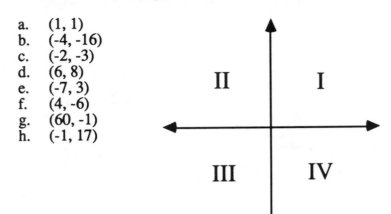

2. Using the diagram below, determine the distance between the following points.

a. (1, 1), (1, 3)
b. (3, 3), (1, 1)
c. (1, 3), (2, -1)
d. (-4, -7), (1, 3)
e. (-4, 1), (2, -1)

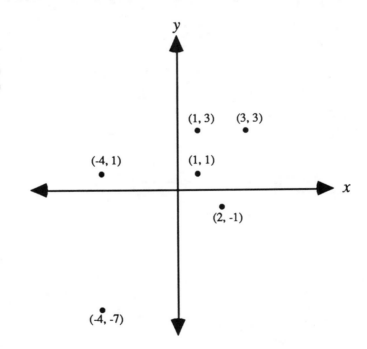

ANSWERS AND EXPLANATIONS—PRACTICE SET 28

1. a. I
   b. III
   c. III
   d. I
   e. II
   f. IV
   g. IV
   h. II

2. a. 2

   Since one of the coordinates is the same for both points (x=1) we can treat this as a distance problem on a numberline:

   $$1 - 3 = -2$$
   $$|-2| = 2$$

   b. $2\sqrt{2}$

   $$d = \sqrt{(x_2 - x_1)^2 + (y_2 - y_1)^2}$$
   $$= \sqrt{(1-3)^2 + (1-3)^2}$$
   $$= \sqrt{(-2)^2 + (-2)^2}$$
   $$= \sqrt{4+4}$$
   $$= \sqrt{8}$$
   $$= 2\sqrt{2}$$

   c. $\sqrt{17}$

   $$d = \sqrt{(x_2 - x_1)^2 + (y_2 - y_1)^2}$$
   $$= \sqrt{(2-1)^2 + (-1-3)^2}$$
   $$= \sqrt{(1)^2 + (-4)^2}$$
   $$= \sqrt{1+16}$$
   $$= \sqrt{17}$$

d. $5\sqrt{5}$

$$d = \sqrt{(x_2 - x_1)^2 + (y_2 - y_1)^2}$$
$$= \sqrt{(1 - -4)^2 + (3 - -7)^2}$$
$$= \sqrt{(5)^2 + (10)^2}$$
$$= \sqrt{25 + 100}$$
$$= \sqrt{125}$$
$$= 5\sqrt{5}$$

e. $2\sqrt{10}$

$$d = \sqrt{(x_2 - x_1)^2 + (y_2 - y_1)^2}$$
$$= \sqrt{(2 - -4)^2 + (-1 - 1)^2}$$
$$= \sqrt{(6)^2 + (-2)^2}$$
$$= \sqrt{36 + 4}$$
$$= \sqrt{40}$$
$$= 2\sqrt{10}$$

Lines and Angles

Lines

If you were to draw a line between points (3, -6) and (-5, 2), you'd have a *line segment*. A line segment is a section of a straight line. Above we called the points point 1 and point 2, but usually they're labeled with a letter, so let's call point 1 point *A*, and point 2 point *B*. Line segments are identified via the letters assigned their endpoints. The line segment below is thus known as line segment *AB*.

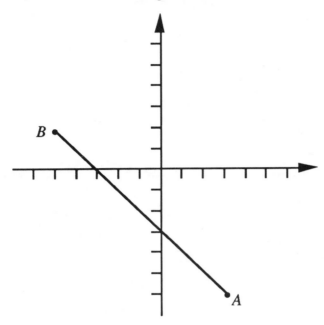

Lines (as opposed to line segments) go on and on forever (hence the arrows that mark their ends).

Single Angles

Lines form *angles*. A straight line forms a *straight*, or 180° angle. Two intersecting lines, or line segments, can form angles of all different degrees. The two axes above are perpendicular to one another because they meet each other at a *right* or 90° angle. Perpendicular lines are indicated via the ⊥ symbol and right angles are denoted via the placement of small square in the seat of the angle. Angles less than 90° are *acute*. Angles more than 90° are *obtuse*. Here's an example of each:

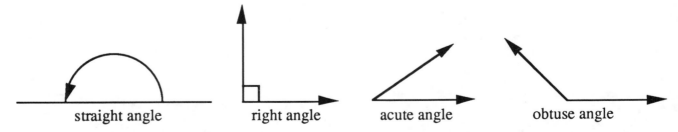

straight angle   right angle   acute angle   obtuse angle

Angles are labeled several different ways. Oftentimes the end of each line segment and the *vertex* (the point of intersection) are marked with upper case letters. Sometimes only the interior of the angle is labeled, and usually with a lower case letter. The angle below could be referred to as either *ABC* or *a*.

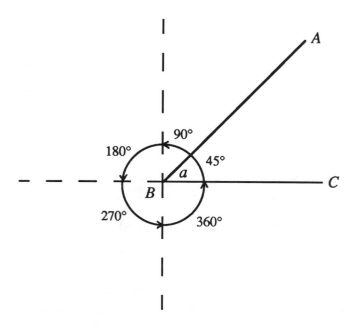

If we opened up a 45° angle to 90° degrees we'd have a right angle. If we opened it up another 90° we'd have a straight angle. Tack on 2 more 90° and we'd have one full revolution, a 360° circle. You can think of angles as fractions of circles. Angles less than 360° are angles that are some fraction of 360°. Our 45° angle represents an eighth of a circle, or $\frac{1}{8}$ 360°.

Adjacent Angles

Angles that share a <u>side</u> and a <u>vertex</u> are *adjacent* angles. Adjacent angles that sum to 90° are *complementary* angles, and adjacent angles that sum to 180° are *supplementary* angles.

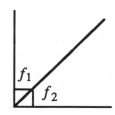

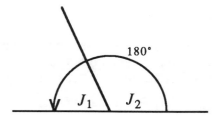

b_1 and b_2 are
adjacent angles

f_1 and f_2 are
complementary angles

J_1 and J_2 are
supplementary angles

Vertical angles are the pairs of opposite angles that are formed when two lines, or line segments, intersect and cross. Vertical (opposite) angles are always equal.

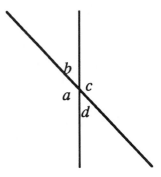

The two pairs of vertical angles, a and c, and b and d, sum to 360° and any two adjacent angles sum to 180°: $a + b = 180°$, $b + c = 180°$, $c + d = 180°$, and $d + a = 180°$. Note that $a + c \neq 180°$ and $b + d \neq 180°$ as they do not fit the definition of adjacent angles. (If the vertical angles are all right angles, then any two angles, of course, would sum to 180°.)

Parallel Lines, Transversals and Angles

Lines in the same plane that will never intersect are parallel lines. $X \parallel Y$ means that line X is parallel to line Y. A line crossing parallel lines is called a *transversal*. In the figure below Z crosses X and Y and is thus a transversal. Many angles (8 to be exact) are formed when a transversal cuts across parallel lines.

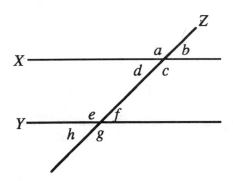

The important thing to remember about transversals of parallel lines is that the four acute angles formed are equal to each other and the four obtuse angles formed are equal to each other. If the transversal is perpendicular, then all eight angles are equal. Otherwise, eyeballing the eight angles usually reveals which angles are acute and which angles are obtuse, and thus which ones are equal.

Put any of the first group of equal angles with any of the second group of equal angles and you've got 180°. In the figure above, each small or acute angle is supplementary to each large or obtuse angle. Knowing the size of any one angle on the figure thus allows you to discern the seven others. If angle $a = 135°$, then angle b must equal $180° - 135° = 45°$. Angles a, c, e and g all equal 135° and angles b, d, f, and h all equal 45°.

Here are a few exercises to sharpen your understanding of these relationships:

1. $P \parallel Q$ is transversed by Y. What is the sum of the 8 angles that are formed?

    The 8 angles form 4 supplementary pairs. So $4 \times 180° = 720°$ is the sum of the 8 angles.

2. $P \parallel Q$ is transversed by Y and Y is $\perp$ to P. How many right angles are formed?

    Y must also be perpendicular to Q. All 8 angles that are formed are 90°, and thus right angles.

3. $P \parallel Q$ is transversed by both Y and Z, and $Y \parallel Z$. If one of the angles formed is 15°, what is the sum of all the other acute angles formed?

    16 angles would be formed all together, 8 acute at 15° apiece, and 8 obtuse at 165° apiece. So $7 \times 15° = 105°$ is the sum of the 7 other acute angles.

PRACTICE SET 29

1.   What are the degree measures of *a*, *b*, and *c* in the diagram below?

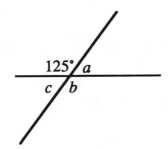

2.   If $R \parallel S$, then what are the degree measures of *a*, *b*, *c*, and *d* in the diagram below?

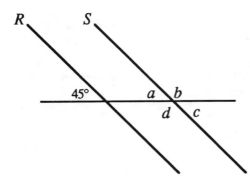

3.   If $X \parallel Y$ and $Z \perp X$, what are the degree measures of *l* and *m* in the diagram below?

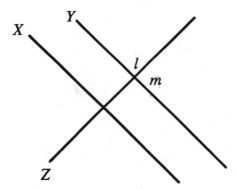

4. If $R \parallel S$ and $T \parallel U$, then what are the degree measures of w, x, y, and z in the diagram below?

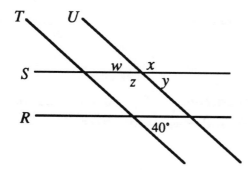

ANSWERS AND EXPLANATIONS—PRACTICE SET 29

1. $a = 55°, b = 125°, c = 55°$

    Angle a is a supplement to the 125° angle so angle $a = 180°-125°= 55°$. By vertical angles $b = 125°, c = 55°$.

2. $a = 45°, b = 135°, c = 45°, d = 135°$

    The four acute angles formed by the transversal are equal so $45° = a = c$. The four obtuse angles formed by the transversal are equal so $180° - 45° = 135° = b = d$.

3. $l = 90°, m = 90°$

    Since X ‖ Y and Z ⊥ X, Y ⊥ Z and l and m are both right angles.

4. $w = 40°, x = 140°, y = 40°, z = 140°$

    Since R‖S and T‖U, all acute angles formed are equal, and all obtuse angles formed are equal. $40° = w = y$ and $180° - 40° = 140° = x = z$.

Polygons

Regular v. Irregular

Polygons are closed plane figures bounded by line segments. Three sided polygons are triangles and four sided polygons are quadrilaterals. Five, six and eight sided polygons are called pentagons, hexagons and octagons, respectively. Polygons are labeled according to the (usually) upper case letters that mark their vertices (points at which the line segments intersect). Polygons can be either *regular* or *irregular*. Regular polygons are polygons in which all of the angles and sides are equal. (An equal number of small dashes through two or more sides indicates that those sides are equal.) Irregular polygons are polygons in which all or some of the angles and sides are not equal.

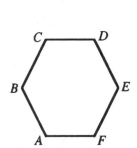
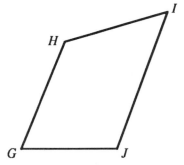

regular hexagon *ABCDEF*   irregular quadrilateral *GHIJ*

Polygons are *congruent* with one another if their corresponding angles and sides are <u>equal</u>. Polygons are *similar* to one another if their corresponding angles are <u>equal</u> and sides are <u>proportional</u>.

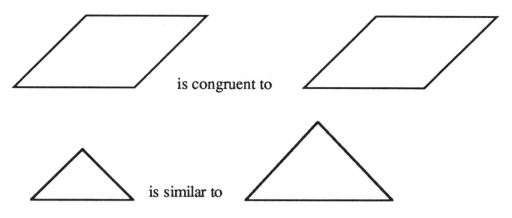

is congruent to

is similar to

Figuring the Sum of Angles

Figuring out how many degrees are inside the angles of a polygon is a simple yet important task. There are two methods you can use:

1. Divide the polygon up into adjacent triangles by adding diagonals until <u>only</u> triangles are inside the polygon. (A quadrilateral would need one diagonal, a pentagon two, a hexagon three, and an octagon five) Count the number of triangles formed and multiply that number by 180° (<u>all</u> triangles add up to 180°).

    or

2. Use the sum of angles formula for an x sided polygon: total degrees $= (x-2)180°$

    Let's try each out with a octagon:

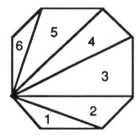

total degrees $= 180°(6)$
$= 1080°$

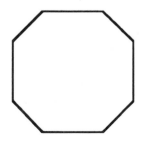

total degrees $= (8-2)180°$
$= (6)180°$
$= 1080°$

Sample Question 45: Assuming the octagon below is regular, what is the measure of 3 of its 8 angles?

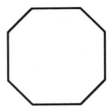

(1) determine the sum of angles

$$\text{total degrees} = (8-2)180°$$
$$= (6)180°$$
$$= 1080°$$

(2) determine the measure of a single angle

$$\begin{array}{r} 135° \\ 8\overline{)1080°} \end{array}$$

(3) multiply the measure of a single angle by the # of angles to be measured

$$135° \times 3 = 405°$$

Figuring Perimeter

The *perimeter* of a figure is the outer boundary of a figure. To figure out the perimeter of a polygon, add the lengths of the sides. This can be accomplished for regular polygons by multiplying the length of one side times the number of sides.

The perimeter of a regular triangle with side 4 would be $4 \times 3 = 12$.
The perimeter of a regular quadrilateral with side 4 would be $4 \times 4 = 16$.
The perimeter of a regular pentagon with side 4 would be $4 \times 5 = 20$.
The perimeter of a regular hexagon with side 4 would be $4 \times 6 = 24$.
The perimeter of a regular octagon with side 4 would be $4 \times 8 = 32$.

Sample Question 46: What is the perimeter of the hexagon formed by the regular triangles if each triangle has a perimeter of 6?

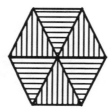

(1) determine the length of a side of the hexagon

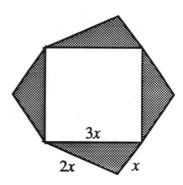

$3\overline{)6}$ with quotient 2 (because each triangle is three sided with a perimeter of six)

(2) multiply side length times # of sides in a hexagon

$2 \times 6 = 12$

Sample Question 47: In the figure below, what is the perimeter of the square formed by the irregular triangles if each of the triangles has a perimeter of 12?

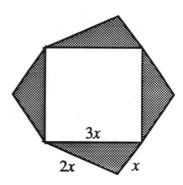

$3x$

$2x$ x

(1) solve for x

$$x + 2x + 3x = 12$$
$$6x = 12$$
$$x = 2$$

(2) determine the length of a side of the square

side $= 3x$
side $= 6$

(3) multiply side length times # of sides in a square

$6 \times 4 = 24$

PRACTICE SET 30

1. What is the sum of the interior angles of the irregular polygon below?

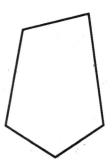

2. Assuming *AB* bisects the regular octagon in the figure below, what is the degree measure of *x*?

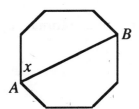

3. A regular polygon has 14 sides. A side is 2 inches. How far is 1/7 the perimeter of the polygon?

216

1. 540°

   total degrees $= (5-2)180°$
   $$= (3)180°$$
   $$= 540°$$

2. 67.50°

   total degrees $= (8-2)180°$
   $$= (6)180°$$
   $$= 1080°$$

   each angle $= \dfrac{1080°}{8} = 135°$

   angle $x = \dfrac{135°}{2} = 67.5°$ ← since AB bisects the regular octagon at a vertex

3. 4 inches

   $14 \times 2 = 28$ inches ← figure perimeter

   $\dfrac{28}{7} = 4$ inches ← perimeter ÷ 7

Triangles

Types of Triangles

In the previous section we said that polygons that have equal angles and sides are regular polygons, and we gave, as an example of a regular polygon, a regular triangle. Regular triangles are also called *equilateral* triangles. Because all triangles sum to 180°, each angle in an equilateral triangle contains 60° (180° ÷ 3 = 60°). In an *isosceles* triangle, two sides and two angles are equal.

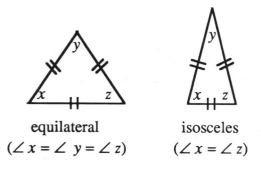

equilateral $(\angle x = \angle y = \angle z)$ isosceles $(\angle x = \angle z)$

Just as there are acute, right and obtuse angles, there are acute, right and obtuse triangles. *Acute* triangles have <u>three</u> acute angles, *right* triangles have <u>one</u> right angle and *obtuse* triangles have <u>one</u> obtuse angle.

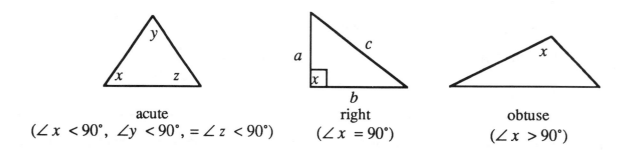

acute $(\angle x < 90°, \angle y < 90°, = \angle z < 90°)$ right $(\angle x = 90°)$ obtuse $(\angle x > 90°)$

Right Triangles

The most important of the above triangles, at least in terms of standardized tests, is the right triangle. In a right triangle, the sides flanking the right angle are the *legs*, and the side opposite the right angle is the *hypotenuse*. Right triangles are special because the sum of the squares of the length of the legs (the two short sides) equals the square of the length of the hypotenuse (the long side). This is usually written as follows:

$a^2 + b^2 = c^2$

So, if you know two of the three sides of a right triangle, you can figure out the third. Recognition of this principle (the Pythagorean Theorem) is widely tested, and usually with the following triplets, or multiples thereof:

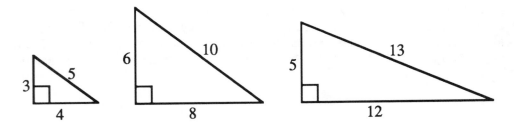

A consideration: You might come across a right triangle with a leg of 40 and a hypotenuse of 50, or one with legs of 12 and 16. These are derivations of the above triplets. Without doing the computations you should recognize that the second leg in the first triangle would be 30, and the hypotenuse in the second triangle would be 20.

Sample Question 48: What is the hypotenuse of a right triangle with sides 9 and 12?

(1) consider possible relation to the common triplets

$$3 \times 3 = 9$$
$$\text{and}$$
$$4 \times 3 = 12$$

(yes, this is a derivitive of the 3-4-5 triangle)

(2) multiply the hypotenuse of the 3-4-5 triangle by the common factor

$$5 \times 3 = 15$$

Sample Question 49: If a right triangle has a hypotenuse of $3\sqrt{5}$ and a side of 3, what's the remaining side?

(1) consider possible relation to the common triplets

not recognizable

(2) use the Pythagorean formula

$$a^2 + b^2 = c^2$$
$$3^2 + b^2 = \left(3\sqrt{5}\right)^2$$
$$9 + b^2 = \left(3\sqrt{5}\right)\left(3\sqrt{5}\right)$$
$$b^2 = 9\sqrt{25} - 9$$
$$b^2 = 9(5) - 9$$
$$b^2 = 45 - 9$$
$$b^2 = 36$$
$$b = \sqrt{36}$$
$$b = 6$$

In two special right triangles, the 45°: 45°: 90° triangle and the 30°: 60°: 90° triangle, the ratio between the length of sides is constant. Therefore, if you know you are dealing with one of these triangles, and if you know the length of any one of the three sides, you can figure out the length of the other sides. Here are the special triangles and their ratios:

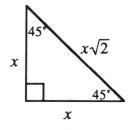
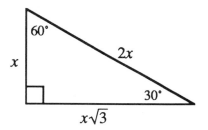

Sample Question 50: An isosceles right triangle has a side of 10. What is it's hypotenuse?

(1) recall the isosceles right triangle ratio

$x : x : x\sqrt{2}$

(2) plug in what's given

$10 : 10 : 10\sqrt{2}$

(3) isolate the hypotenuse

hypotenuse = $10\sqrt{2}$

The "1 Exterior = 2 Interior" Principle

The three angles inside triangles are called *interior* angles and each interior angle is supplemented by an *exterior* angle (see below). If $\angle c$ in the triangle below is equal to 45°, then the remaining 2 angles, $\angle a$ and $\angle b$ must together equal 180° − 45° = 135°, and so must the exterior angle adjacent to $\angle c$. This demonstrates the principle that the supplementary exterior angles are equal to the sum of the two interior angles that they are *not* adjacent to. Additionally, the supplementary exterior angles of any triangle must sum to 360°. (Interior angles = 180°, and each interior angle, combined with its adjacent supplementary exterior angle = 180°. So 180° × 3 − 180° = the sum of the exterior supplementary angles.)

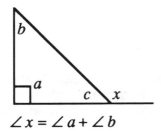

$$\angle x = \angle a + \angle b$$

Sample Question 51: If $b = (2)c$, what's the value of $\angle d$?

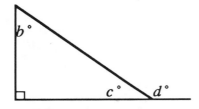

(1) determine the values of $\angle b$ and $\angle c$

$$180° - 90° = 90°$$
$$b + c = 90$$
$$2c + c = 90$$
$$3c = 90$$
$$c = 30$$
so
$$\angle c = 30° \text{ and } \angle b = 60°$$

(2) determine the value of $\angle d$ by subtracting $\angle c$ from 180°

$$180° - 30° = 150°$$

Angle/Side Properties

Here are a few things to remember about the angles and sides of triangles:

1. In all triangles, the three interior angles sum to 180° and the three supplementary exterior angles sum to 360°.

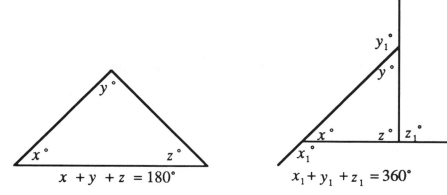

$$x + y + z = 180°$$

$$x_1 + y_1 + z_1 = 360°$$

2. Given two unequal sides in a triangle, the longer side is always opposite the larger angle and vice versa.

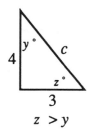

$$z > y$$

3. The length of any one side is less than the sum of the lengths of the other two sides. Another way of saying this is that the length of any one side is greater than the difference between the lengths of the other two sides.

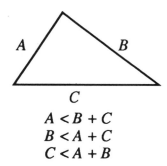

$$A < B + C$$
$$B < A + C$$
$$C < A + B$$

4. If two sides are of equal length, then the triangle is an isosceles (and the angles opposite the equal sides are themselves equal.)

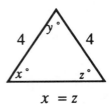

$$x = z$$

5. If two angles are equal, then the triangle is an isosceles (and the sides opposite the equal angles are themselves equal.)

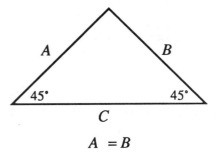

$$A = B$$

6. If two triangles (*ABE* and *ACD*) share an angle, the sums of the other two angles are equal.

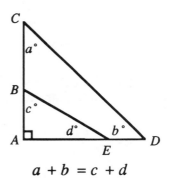

$$a + b = c + d$$

Figuring Area

To find the area of a triangle use the formula:

$$\text{area} = \frac{1}{2}(\text{base})(\text{height})$$

The base of a triangle is simply any one of the sides, and the height is simply the altitude measured at a right angle to the base, which may be a leg (in the case of right triangles), inside the triangle (in the case of acute triangles), or outside the triangle (in the case of obtuse triangles). Here's an example of each:

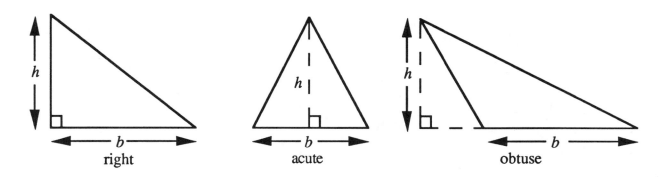

Sample Question 52: What is the area of $\triangle ACE$ if the area of $\triangle ABC$ is $2\frac{1}{2}$ and the area of $\triangle CDE$ is 6?

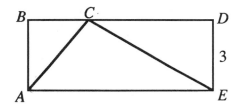

(1) determine the base and the height of the rectangle

$$\text{height} = \text{length of } DE = 3$$
$$\text{base} = BC + CD$$

$$\triangle ABC = \frac{1}{2}(\text{base})(\text{height})$$

$$\triangle ABC = \frac{1}{2}(BC)(3)$$

$$\frac{5}{2} = \frac{1}{2}(3BC)$$

$$\frac{5}{2} = \frac{3BC}{2}$$

$$BC = \frac{10}{6}$$

$$= \frac{5}{3}$$

$$\Delta CDE = \frac{1}{2}(\text{base})(\text{height})$$

$$\Delta CDE = \frac{1}{2}(CD)(3)$$

$$6 = \frac{1}{2}(3CD)$$

$$6 = \frac{3CD}{2}$$

$$\left(\frac{2}{3}\right)6 = CD$$

$$CD = 4$$

$$\text{base} = \frac{5}{3} + 4$$

$$= \frac{5}{3} + \frac{12}{3}$$

$$= \frac{17}{3}$$

(2) use the area formula

$$\text{area} = \frac{1}{2}(\text{base})(\text{height})$$

$$\text{area } \Delta ACE = \frac{1}{2}\left(\frac{17}{3}\right)(3)$$

$$= \frac{17}{2}$$

Sample Question 53: Given that the area of ΔEBD is 12, what are the areas of the shaded triangles ΔABE and ΔBCD?

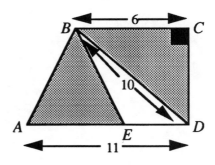

(1) determine the base and height of ΔBCD

$$\text{base} = 6(\text{given})$$

$$\text{height} = 8(\text{this is a } 6\text{-}8\text{-}10 \text{ right } \Delta)$$

(2) determine the area of $\triangle BCD$

$$\text{area } \triangle BCD = \frac{1}{2}(\text{base})(\text{height})$$

$$= \frac{1}{2}(6)(8)$$

$$= \frac{1}{2}(48)$$

$$= \frac{48}{2}$$

$$= 24$$

(3) determine the base and height of $\triangle ABE$

$$\text{base} = 11 - ED$$
$$\text{height} = 8$$

$$\text{area } \triangle EBD = \frac{1}{2}(\text{base})(\text{height})$$

$$12 = \frac{1}{2}(ED)(8)$$

$$12 = \frac{1}{2}(8ED)$$

$$12 = \frac{8ED}{2}$$

$$12 = 4ED$$

$$ED = \frac{12}{4}$$

$$= 3$$

$$\text{base} = 11 - 3 = 8$$
$$\text{height} = 8$$

(4) determine the area of $\triangle ABE$

$$\text{area } \triangle ABE = \frac{1}{2}(\text{base})(\text{height})$$

$$= \frac{1}{2}(8)(8)$$

$$= \frac{1}{2}(64)$$

$$= 32$$

PRACTICE SET 31

1. What is the length x in the triangle below?

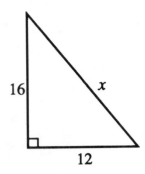

2. What is the value of length Z in the triangle below?

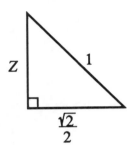

3. What is the value of a in the triangle below?

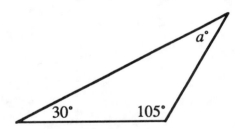

4. What is the value of y in the figure below?

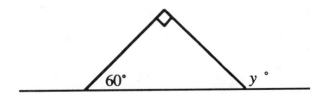

5.   Which side of the triangle below is the longest?

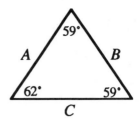

6.   What are the values of x and y?

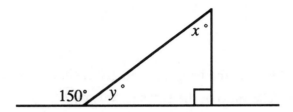

7.   a. What is the area of the triangle *ABC* shown below?
     b. What is the perimeter of the triangle *ABC*?

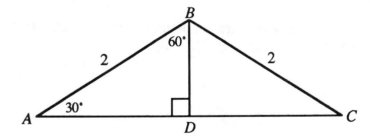

ANSWERS AND EXPLANATIONS—PRACTICE SET 31

1. **20** This triangle is similar to the 3-4-5 right triangle:

    $3 \times 4 = 12$

    $4 \times 4 = 16$

    $5 \times 4 = 20$

    Or by Pythagorean:

    $$a^2 + b^2 = c^2$$
    $$12^2 + 16^2 = c^2$$
    $$144 + 256 = c^2$$
    $$400 = c^2$$
    $$x = 20$$

2. $\frac{\sqrt{2}}{2}$ This triangle is a $45°{:}45°{:}90°$ triangle because the length of the given side multiplied by $\sqrt{2}$ gives the length of the hypotenuse. The ratio of the sides is $x{:}x{:}x\sqrt{2}$.

3. **45** The interior angles of a triangle add to 180: $a = 180 - 30 - 105 = 180 - 135 = 45$.

4. **150** Supplementary exterior angles are equal to the sum of the two interior angles they are not adjacent to so $y = 90 + 60 = 150$.

5. **B** The side opposite the largest angle is longest.

6. **$x = 60$, $y = 30$** Angle y and its exterior angle are supplements, so $y = 180 - 150 = 30$. The angles in a triangle sum to 180 so $x = 180 - 90 - 30 = 60$.

7. a. $\sqrt{3}$

    b. $4 + 2\sqrt{3}$

    Because AB = BC, ABC is an isosceles triangle, angle A = angle C and angle ADB = angle BDC. We have two $30°{:}60°{:}90°$ triangles so the ratio of the length of the sides is as follows: $x{:}x\sqrt{3}{:}2x$

Since $2x = 2$ in our triangles, $x = 1$, DB = 1, DC = $\sqrt{3}$ and AD=$\sqrt{3}$.

$$\text{area} = \frac{1}{2}(\text{base})(\text{height})$$

$$= \frac{1}{2}(2\sqrt{3})(1) \leftarrow \text{length of entire base is } 2\sqrt{3}$$

$$= \frac{2\sqrt{3}}{2}$$

$$= \sqrt{3}$$

$$\text{perimeter} = 2 + 2 + 2\sqrt{3}$$

$$= 4 + 2\sqrt{3}$$

Quadrilaterals

Types of Quadrilaterals

Quadrilaterals are 4-sided polygons. The 4 interior angles of quadrilaterals always sum to 360°. (Quadrilaterals split into 2 triangles and $2 \times 180° = 360°$.) Below are the five common types of quadrilaterals.

1. A *trapezoid* is a quadrilateral with exactly two sides parallel.

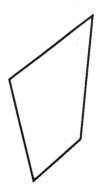

2. A *parallelogram* is a quadrilateral with opposite sides both equal and parallel.

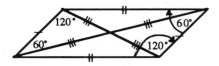

opposite angles are equal
adjacent angles are supplementary
diagonals bisect one another

3. A *rhombus* is a parallelogram with all sides equal.

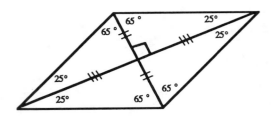

opposite angles are equal
adjacent angles are supplementary
diagonals bisect one another
diagonals are perpendicular to one another
diagonals bisect the angles they connect

4. A *rectangle* is a parallelogram with four right angles.

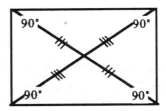

opposite angles are equal
adjacent angles are supplementary
diagonals bisect one another
diagonals are equal

5. A *square* is a rectangle with four equal sides.

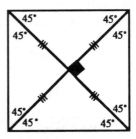

opposite angles are equal
adjacent angles are supplementary
diagonals bisect one another
diagonals are perpendicular to one another
diagonals bisect the angles they connect
diagonals are equal

(A consideration: rhombuses, rectangles and squares are all parallelograms, and there-fore opposite sides are both equal and parallel.)

Sample Question 54: What is the area of the shaded region in the square below?

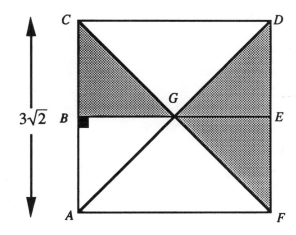

(1) determine the area of $\triangle CBG$

Because BE bisects the square and the square has a side of $3\sqrt{2}$, BG and BC must be half a side, or $\frac{3\sqrt{2}}{2}$.

$$\text{area } \triangle CBG = \frac{1}{2}(BG)(BC)$$
$$= \frac{1}{2}\left(\frac{3\sqrt{2}}{2}\right)\left(\frac{3\sqrt{2}}{2}\right)$$
$$= \frac{9}{4}$$

(2) determine total area

Because $\triangle CBG$, $\triangle DEG$ and $\triangle FEG$ are all congruent, the total area is simply three times the area of $\triangle CBG$.

$$3\left(\frac{9}{4}\right) = \frac{27}{4} \text{ or } 6\frac{3}{4}$$

Figuring Area

(1) To find the area of a trapezoid use the formula:

$$\text{area of a trapezoid} = \left(\frac{\text{base}_1 + \text{base}_2}{2}\right)(\text{height})$$

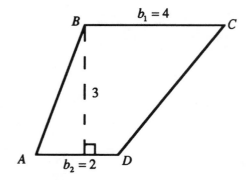

$$\text{area } ABCD = \left(\frac{4+2}{2}\right)(3)$$

$$= \left(\frac{6}{2}\right)(3)$$

$$= \frac{18}{2}$$

$$= 9$$

(2) To find the area of a parallelogram use the formula:

area of a parallelogram = (base)(height)

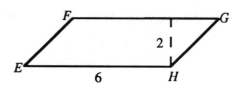

$$\text{area } EFGH = (6)(2)$$

$$= 12$$

(3) To find the area of a rectangle use the formula:

area of a rectangle = (length)(width)

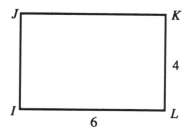

area $IJKL = (6)(4)$
$\qquad = 24$

(4) To find the area of a square use the formula:

area of a square = $(\text{side})^2$

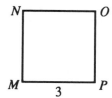

area $MNOP = (3)^2$
$\qquad = 9$

A consideration: The rectangle and square formulas are simply derivations of the parallelogram formula. (Rectangles and squares *are* parallelograms.)

Sample Question 55: Given that the area of parallelogram *ABCH* is 28 and that the area of trapezoid *GCDE* is 18 what are the areas of *GCDF*, $\triangle HCG$ and *ABDF*?

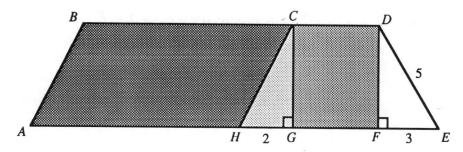

(1) determine the width (or height) of *GCDF* (and thus the height of each polygon in the figure)

right $\triangle FDE$ is a 3-4-5 triplet
height = 4

(2) determine the length of CD and GF with the formula for the area of a trapezoid
If $CD = x$, then $GE = x + 3$.

$$\text{area of trapezoid } GCDE = (4)\left(\frac{(x)+(x+3)}{2}\right)$$

$$18 = (4)\left(\frac{(x)+(x+3)}{2}\right)$$

$$18 = (4)\left(\frac{2x+3}{2}\right)$$

$$18 = 2(2x+3)$$

$$18 = 4x+6$$

$$12 = 4x$$

$$x = \frac{12}{4}$$

$$= 3$$

(3) determine the area of the rectangle $GCDF$

$$\text{area of } GCDF = (3)(4)$$

$$= 12$$

(4) determine the area of $\triangle HCG$

$$\text{area of } \triangle HCG = \frac{1}{2}(2)(4)$$

$$= \frac{1}{2}(8)$$

$$= \frac{8}{2}$$

$$= 4$$

(5) add the areas of $ABCH$, $\triangle HCG$, and $GCDF$ to determine the area of $ABDF$

$$28 + 4 + 12 = 44$$

Sample Question 56: Given that *ABCE* is a square, and that Δ*AFE* is an isosceles triangle, what are the areas of *AFDE* and *ABCE*?

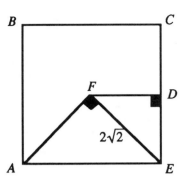

(1) determine the length of *AE* (and thus a side of the square)

Δ*AFE* is a 45°: 45°: 90° triangle (because angle *AFE* equals 90°, angles *A* and *E* are bisected and thus create four 45° angles)

$$\text{sides ratio} = x:x:x\sqrt{2} \text{ for leg: leg: hypotenuse}$$
$$\text{sides ratio} = 2\sqrt{2}:2\sqrt{2}:\left(2\sqrt{2}\right)\sqrt{2}$$
$$\text{length of } AE = \left(2\sqrt{2}\right)\sqrt{2}$$
$$= 2\sqrt{4}$$
$$= 2(2)$$
$$= 4$$

(2) determine the area of square *ABCE*

$$\text{area of a square} = (\text{side})^2$$
$$\text{area of } ABCE = 4^2$$
$$= 16$$

(3) determine the area of Δ*FDE*

Δ*FDE* is a 45°: 45°: 90° triangle (angle *E* is bisected)

$$\text{sides ratio} = x:x:x\sqrt{2} \text{ for leg: leg: hypotenuse}$$
$$\text{sides ratio} = 2:2:2\sqrt{2}$$
$$\text{area} = \frac{1}{2}bh$$
$$\text{area of } \Delta FDE = \frac{1}{2}(2)(2)$$
$$= 2$$

(4) determine the area of $\triangle AFE$

$$\text{area} = \frac{1}{2}bh$$

$$\text{area of } \triangle AFE = \frac{1}{2}(2)(4)$$

$$= 4$$

(5) add the area of $\triangle FDE$ and $\triangle AFE$

$$2 + 4 = 6$$

$$\text{area } AFDE = 6$$

PRACTICE SET 32

1. What is the area and the perimeter of the square shown below?

3

2. In terms of x, what is the area and the perimeter of the rectangle shown below?

4x

2x

3. In the figure below, if the diagonal DB has a length of 2, what is the area and the perimeter of the square $ABCD$?

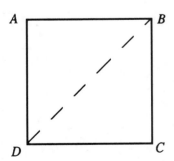

4. In the figure below, length $BE = 2\sqrt{3}$ and length $EC = 4\sqrt{3}$. What is the area and the perimeter of the parallelogram $ACDE$?

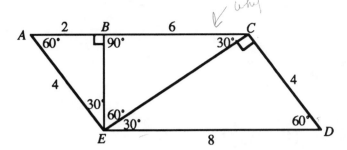

5. $QRTU$ is a square and length $QU = 3$. What is the area of the trapezoid $QRSV$?

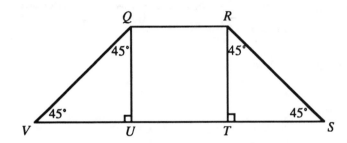

ANSWERS AND EXPLANATIONS—PRACTICE SET 32

1. area = 9, perimeter = 12

   area of a square = $s^2 = 3^2 = 9$

   perimeter of a square = $4(\text{side}) = 4(3) = 12$

2. area = $8x^2$, perimeter = $12x$

   area of a rectangle = $(\text{length})(\text{width}) = (4x)(2x) = 8x^2$

   perimeter of a rectangle = $2(\text{length}) + 2(\text{width}) = 2(4x) + 2(2x) = 8x + 4x = 12x$

3. area = 2, perimeter = $4\sqrt{2}$

   Diagonal DB cuts the square into 2 45°:45°:90° triangles, each with a hypotenuse of length 2. Since the ratio of the length of the sides of a 45°:45°:90° triangle is $x:x:x\sqrt{2}$:

   $x\sqrt{2} = 2 \leftarrow$ solve for x to find the length of a side

   $$x = \frac{2}{\sqrt{2}}$$

   $$= \frac{2}{\sqrt{2}}\left(\frac{\sqrt{2}}{\sqrt{2}}\right) \leftarrow \text{rationalize the denominator}$$

   $$= \frac{2\sqrt{2}}{2}$$

   $$= \sqrt{2}$$

   Now compute the area and the perimeter of the square:

   area = $\text{side}^2 = \sqrt{2}^2 = 2$

   perimeter = $4(side) = 4\left(\sqrt{2}\right) = 4\sqrt{2}$

4. area = $16\sqrt{3}$, perimeter = 24

   area of a parallelogram = $(\text{base})(\text{height})$
   $$= 8\left(2\sqrt{3}\right)$$
   $$= 16\sqrt{3}$$

$$\text{perimeter of a parallelogram} = 2(\text{base}_1) + 2(\text{base}_2)$$
$$= 2(8) + 2(4)$$
$$= 16 + 8$$
$$= 24$$

5. area = 18

The two triangles are isosceles with legs of 3 so the bottom base = $3 + 3 + 3 = 9$.

$$\text{area of a trapezoid} = \left(\frac{b_1 + b_2}{2}\right)(\text{height})$$
$$= \left(\frac{3 + 9}{2}\right)(3)$$
$$= (6)(3)$$
$$= 18$$

Circles

Circle Parts

A *circle* is a closed curve made up of a series of points which are all equidistant from a certain point, or the *center* of the circle. The distance around a circle is the *circumference*, and the distance from any point on the circumference to the center of a circle is the *radius*. Twice the distance of the radius equals the *diameter*, or the distance across the center of the circle.

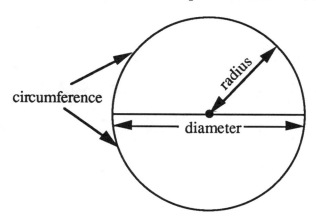

A *chord* is a line segment whose end points lie somewhere on the circumference. Diameters are a type of chord. A *secant* is a line or line segment that cuts through a circle by intersecting the circumference at two points. A *semicircle* is a half-circle. An *arc* is a section of the circumference. A semicircle is a kind of arc. A *tangent* is a line or line segment outside a circle that touches the circumference at exactly one point. A radius that springs from the point at which a tangent intersects a circumference lies at a right angle to the tangent.

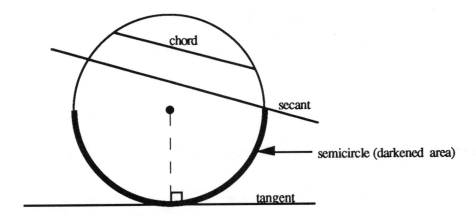

An angle inside a circle made up of two radii is a *central* angle and an angle inside a circle made up of two chords that intersect at an end point is an *inscribed* angle. A *sector* is the area of a circle between two radii.

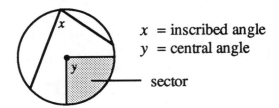

x = inscribed angle
y = central angle

— sector

Circumference

The ratio of the circumference of a circle to a circle's diameter is constant, and is slightly larger than 3.14. This ratio is called pi (π). The formula for the circumference of a circle is thus derived as follows:

$$\frac{\text{circumference}}{\text{diameter}} = \pi$$

circumference = $\pi \times$ diameter

circumference = $2\pi r$ (where r = radius)

The circumference of a circle with a radius of 4 then, would be 8π, and the circumference of a circle with a diameter of 4 would be 4π.

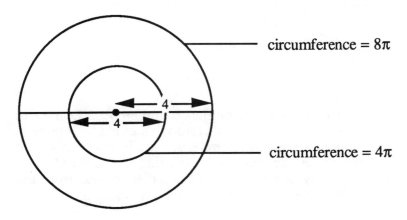

circumference = 8π

circumference = 4π

Sample Question 57: *AC* is tangent to the circle. Which is greater, the circumference of the circle centered at *B*, or the perimeter of square *ABCE*?

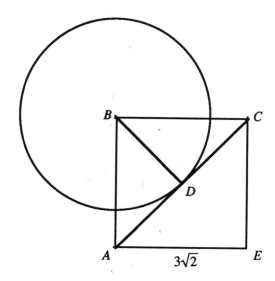

(1) determine the perimeter of *ABCE*

$$\text{perimeter of } ABCE = 4 \times 3\sqrt{2}$$
$$= 12\sqrt{2}$$
$$\approx 12 \times 1.4$$
$$\approx 17$$

(2) determine the length of the radius *BD* (*AC* is $\perp$ to *BD*)

$$\triangle ABD = 45° : 45° : 90° \text{ triangle}$$
sides ratio $= x : x : x\sqrt{2}$ for leg: leg: hypotenuse
sides ratio $= 3 : 3 : 3\sqrt{2}$
length of *BD* $= 3$

(3) determine the circumference of circle *B*

$$\text{circumference } B = 2\pi r$$
$$= 2\pi 3$$
$$= 6\pi$$
$$\approx 6(3.14)$$
$$\approx 18.8$$

(4) compare the two areas

$17 < 18.8$ so the circumference of circle *B* > the perimeter of square *ABCE*

Arc Length and Central Angles

Arcs have the same <u>degree</u> measure (as opposed to length measure) as the degree measure of the <u>central</u> angle from which they're created. (The arc defined by a central angle that measures 360° <u>is</u> a circle.) A central angle of 72° forms an arc of 72°, and because 72 is $\frac{1}{5}$ of 360, the arc length is $\frac{1}{5}$ of the circumference of the circle. In the figure below arc *MNO* is 90°, because ∠L is 90°. Also ∠L represents $\frac{1}{4}$ of the degrees in the circle and *MNO* represents $\frac{1}{4}$ of the length of the circumference of the circle.

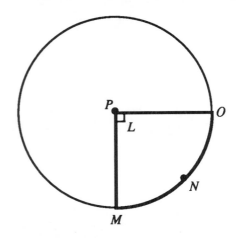

Here's how the formula looks:

$$\text{arc length} = \frac{\text{degrees of central angle}}{360} \text{ (circumference of circle)}$$

If the circumference of the circle above is 8π, the arc *MNO* must measure $\frac{1}{4}$ of 8π, or 2π.

Sample Question 58: If the circumference of the circle below is 15π, what is the combined length of the arcs of the unshaded sectors?

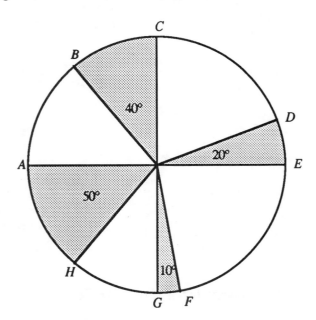

(1) add together the angles in the shaded sectors and subtract the sum from 360° to determine the unshaded angle sum

$$50 + 40 + 20 + 10 = 120$$
$$360 - 120 = 240$$

degrees of arcs in unshaded sectors = 240

(2) plug the result into the formula for arc length

$$\text{combined arc length} = \left(\frac{240}{360}\right)15\pi$$
$$= \left(\frac{2}{3}\right)15\pi$$
$$= \frac{30\pi}{3}$$
$$= 10\pi$$

Arc Length and Inscribed Angles

Arcs created by *inscribed* angles, on the other hand, are twice the size of the inscribed angles from which they're created. Here's the inscribed angle formula:

$$\text{arc length} = \frac{2 \text{ (degrees of inscribed angle)}}{360} \text{ (circumference of circle)}$$

In the example below, the inscribed angle x measures 30°, and the arc ABC created by it measures 60°. If the circumference of the circle were 30π, the length of the arc created by the inscribed circle would be 5π.

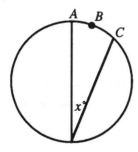

Be able to work these formulas in the reverse, too. Say an 45° angle inscribed in a circle T creates an arc BCD that measures 7π. What would be the circumference of circle T? Well, arc BCD must measure twice the inscribed angle, or 90°, and thus represents $\frac{1}{4}$ of the length of the entire circumference. The circumference of circle T, then, is $7\pi \times 4$ or 28π.

Sample Question 59: If $y = 60°$ and the length of arc $CDE = \frac{10}{3}\pi$, what is the circumference of the circle?

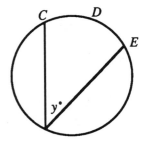

(1) determine the degree measure of arc CDE

$$60° \times 2 = 120°$$

(2) determine the fraction of the measurement of the circumference that arc CDE represents

$$\text{arc } CDE = \frac{120}{360}$$

$$= \frac{12}{36}$$

$$= \frac{1}{3}$$

(3) determine the circumference by multiplying the arc length given by the total parts of the circle

$$\text{circumference} = 3 \times \frac{10}{3}\pi$$

$$= 10\pi$$

A consideration: Usually answers will be left in terms of π. If you are asked to compare two quantities, you need to remember that $\pi \approx 3.14 > 3$. So, for instance, $3\pi > 3^2$.

Figuring the Area of a Circle

The area of a circle = πr^2. The area of a circle with a radius of 3 would be 9π, and the area of a circle with a diameter of 3 would be $\frac{9}{4}\pi$, because a diameter of 3 means a radius of $\frac{3}{2}$.

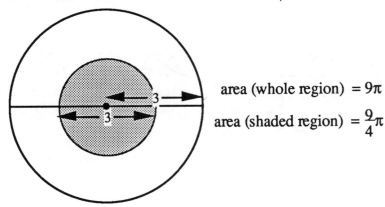

area (whole region) = 9π

area (shaded region) = $\frac{9}{4}\pi$

Sample Question 60: What are the areas of the circles with circumferences 2π, 4π and 6π below?

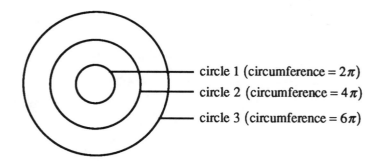

circle 1 (circumference $= 2\pi$)
circle 2 (circumference $= 4\pi$)
circle 3 (circumference $= 6\pi$)

(1) determine the radii of the three circles with the formula for circumference

$$2\pi r = 2\pi$$
$$r = 1$$

$$2\pi r = 4\pi$$
$$r = \frac{4\pi}{2\pi}$$
$$r = 2$$

$$2\pi r = 6\pi$$
$$r = \frac{6\pi}{2\pi}$$
$$r = 3$$

(2) determine the area of the circles with the area formula

area circle 1 $= \pi 1^2$
area circle 1 $= \pi$

area circle 2 $= \pi 2^2$
area circle 2 $= 4\pi$

area circle 3 $= \pi 3^2$
area circle 3 $= 9\pi$

Figuring the Area of a Sector

Recall that sectors are areas created by central angles. To figure the area of a sector of a circle, multiply the fraction of the area of the circle that the sector represents by the area of the circle. Here's the area of a sector formula:

$$\text{area of a sector} = \frac{\text{degrees of central angle}}{360°} \times \pi r^2$$

In the circle below, x measures 90°, and the radius is 5. The area of the whole circle is $\pi 5^2$, or 25π. The area of the sector, then, is $\left(\dfrac{90}{360}\right)25\pi = \dfrac{1}{4}25\pi = \dfrac{25\pi}{4}$.

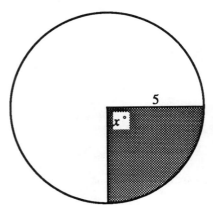

PRACTICE SET 33

1. What is the circumference of a circle with radius 5?

2. What is the area of a circle with radius 5?

3. What is the radius of a circle with circumference 36π?

4. What is the area of a circle with circumference 36π?

5. In the figure below, the arc ABC has an arc length that is 1/8 the circumference of the circle. If the circle is centered at O, then what is the value of x?

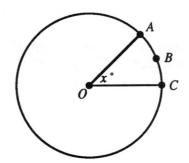

6. In the figure below, the circle centered at O has a circumference of 16π. QR is tangent to the circle. What is the arc length of the arc PSR?

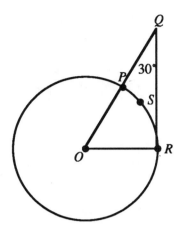

7. If the radius of the circle in the figure below is 2, what is the arc length of the arc XYZ?

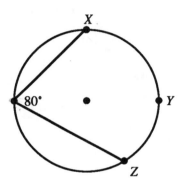

248

ANSWERS AND EXPLANATIONS—PRACTICE SET 33

1. 10π

    circumference $= 2\pi r$
    $= 2\pi(5)$
    $= 10\pi$

2. 25π

    area $= \pi r^2$
    $= \pi(5)^2$
    $= 25\pi$

3. 18

    circumference $= 2\pi r$
    $36\pi = 2\pi r$
    $\dfrac{36\pi}{2\pi} = r$
    $18 = r$

4. 324π

    circumference $= 2\pi r$
    $36\pi = 2\pi r$
    $\dfrac{36\pi}{2\pi} = r$
    $18 = r$

    area $= \pi r^2$
    $= \pi(18)^2$
    $= 324\pi$

5. 45 Since arcs have the same degree measure as the degree measure of the central angle from which they are created:

    x = degree measure of arc ABC
    $= \dfrac{1}{8}(360)$
    $= 45$

6. $\frac{8}{3}\pi$ Since QR is tangent to the circle, QR is perpendicular to OR and angle QOR is $60°$. Use the arc length formula for central angles:

$$\text{arc length} = \frac{\text{degrees of central angle}}{360}(\text{circumference of circle})$$

$$= \frac{60}{360}(16\pi)$$

$$= \frac{16\pi}{6}$$

$$= \frac{8}{3}\pi$$

7. $\frac{16\pi}{9}$ Since the circle has a radius of 2, it has a circumference of 4π. Use the arc length formula for inscribed angles:

$$\text{arc length} = \frac{2(\text{degrees of inscribed angle})}{360}(\text{circumference of circle})$$

$$= \frac{2(80)}{360}(4\pi)$$

$$= \frac{640\pi}{360}$$

$$= \frac{16\pi}{9}$$

Uniform Solids

Rectangular Solids and Cubes

There are three types of uniform solids with which you should be familiar. The first type (of which the second is derivative) is the *rectangular* solid. Compact disc containers are rectangular solids, and so are books. The surface area of a rectangular solid is made up of six rectangles, each of which mirrors the rectangle exactly opposite it. Naturally, all six faces of a rectangular solid meet at right angles. If all six faces of a rectangular solid are equal-sized squares, the rectangular solid is a *cube*, the second type of uniform solid you may encounter. The third type of uniform solid to look out for is the right circular cylinder. The two bases of a right circular cylinder are circles of equal size and are parallel to one another, separated by the height or length of the cylinder. Soft drink cans are right circular cylinders.

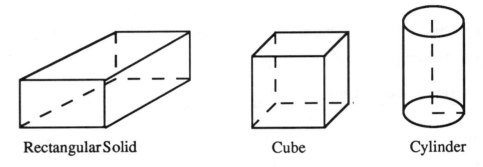

Rectangular Solid   Cube   Cylinder

Figuring Volume

The volume of a uniform solid equals the *area* of the base of the solid times the height of the solid.

Volume of a rectangular solid = length × width × height

Volume of a cube = side^3

Volume of a right circular cylinder = (area of a circle) (height)

The rectangular solid below therefore has a volume of $5 \times 4 \times 3 = 60$, and the cube has a volume of $5^3 = 25(5) = 125$. The right circular cylinder has a volume of $\pi(3^2)9 = \pi(9)9 = 81\pi$.

A Consideration: The labeling of the length, width and height of a rectangle is fairly arbitrary. It doesn't matter which side[s] you call which. Just make sure you use *one* of *each* of the *different* sides in your computations.

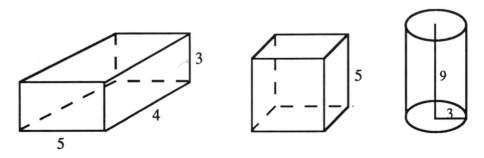

Figuring Surface Area

The surface area of a uniform solid equals the sum of the areas of each of the solid's surfaces or faces.

Surface area of a rectangular solid = 2(length × width) + 2(length × height) + 2(width × height)

Surface area of a cube = 6side^2

Surface area of a right circular cylinder = 2(area of circle) + (circumference)(height)

The rectangular solid above therefore has a surface area of 2(5 × 4) + 2(5 × 3) + 2(4 × 3) = 2(20) + 2(15) + 2(12) = 40 + 30 + 24 = 94, and the cube has a surface area of $6 \times 5^2 = 6(25) = 150$. The right circular cylinder has a surface area of $2(\pi 3^2) + 2\pi 3(9) = 18\pi + 54\pi = 72\pi$.

PRACTICE SET 34

1. What is the surface area and volume of the cube shown below?

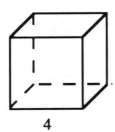

4

2. What is the surface area and volume of the rectangular solid shown below?

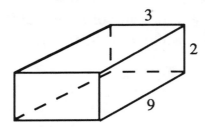

3

2

9

3. What is the surface area and volume of the rectangular solid shown below?

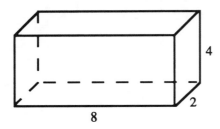

4

2

8

4. The cube below has a surface area of 150. What is the value of x?

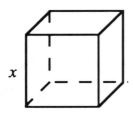

x

5. If the volume of the rectangular solid pictured below is 48, what is the value of x?

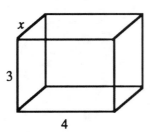

x

3

4

6. What is the volume of the circular cylinder shown below?

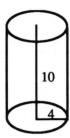

7. What is the surface area of the circular cylinder shown below?

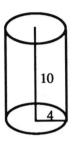

ANSWERS AND EXPLANATIONS—PRACTICE SET 34

1. surface area = 96, volume = 64

$$\text{surface area of a cube} = 6\,\text{side}^2$$
$$= 6(4)^2$$
$$= 6(16)$$
$$= 96$$

$$\text{volume of a cube} = \text{side}^3$$
$$= 4^3$$
$$= 64$$

2. surface area = 102, volume = 54

$$\text{surface area of a rectangular solid} = 2(l \times w) + 2(l \times h) + 2(w \times h)$$
$$= 2(9 \times 3) + 2(9 \times 2) + 2(3 \times 2)$$
$$= 2(27) + 2(18) + 2(6)$$
$$= 54 + 36 + 12$$
$$= 102$$

$$\text{volume of a rectangular solid} = l \times w \times h$$
$$= 9 \times 3 \times 2$$
$$= 54$$

3. surface area = 112, volume = 64

$$\text{surface area of a rectangular solid} = 2(l \times w) + 2(l \times h) + 2(w \times h)$$
$$= 2(8 \times 2) + 2(8 \times 4) + 2(2 \times 4)$$
$$= 2(16) + 2(32) + 2(8)$$
$$= 32 + 64 + 16$$
$$= 112$$

$$\text{volume of a rectangular solid} = l \times w \times h$$
$$= 8 \times 2 \times 4$$
$$= 64$$

4. 5

$$6\,\text{side}^2 = 150$$
$$\text{side}^2 = \frac{150}{6}$$
$$\text{side} = \sqrt{25}$$
$$\text{side} = 5$$

5. 4

$$48 = l \times w \times h$$
$$48 = 4 \times (x) \times 3$$
$$48 = 12x$$
$$x = 4$$

6. volume $= 160\pi$

volume of a right circular cylinder $=$ (area of circle)(height)
$$= \left(\pi r^2\right)(h)$$
$$= \left(\pi 4^2\right)(10)$$
$$= 160\,\pi$$

7. surface area $= 112\pi$

surface area of a right circular cylinder $=$ 2(area of circle) $+$ (circumference)(height)
$$= 2\left(\pi r^2\right) + 2\pi r(\text{height})$$
$$= 2(\pi 16) + 2\pi 40$$
$$= 32\pi + 80\pi$$
$$= 112\,\pi$$